Remix

The Electronic Music Explosion

Written by Bruce M. Gerrish

Edited by Craig Anderton

236 Georgia Street, Suite 100
Vallejo, CA 94590

Library of Congress Catalog Card Number: 00-100535

Art Director: Stephen Ramirez
Cover Design: Linda Gough
Cover Photography: Susana Millman, Coverage Photography (San Francisco, CA)
Book Design and Layout: Linda Gough
Publisher: Mike Lawson
Editorial Director: Patrick Runkle; Associate Editor: Jessica Westcott

EMBooks is an imprint of artistpro.com, LLC
236 Georgia Street, Suite 100
Vallejo, CA 94590
707-554-1935

Also from EMBooks

The Independent Working Musician
Making the Ultimate Demo, 2nd Ed.
Anatomy of a Home Studio
The EM Guide to the Roland VS-880

Also from MixBooks

The AudioPro Home Recording Course, Volumes I, II, and III
I Hate the Man Who Runs This Bar!
The Mastering Engineer's Handbook
Making Music with Your Computer, 2nd Ed.
How to Make Money Scoring Soundtracks and Jingles
The Art of Mixing: A Visual Guide to Recording, Engineering, and Production
500 Songwriting Ideas (For Brave and Passionate People)
Music Publishing: The Real Road to Music Business Success, Rev. and Exp. 5th Ed.
How to Run a Recording Session
Mix Reference Disc, Deluxe Ed.
The Songwriters Guide to Collaboration, Rev. and Exp. 2nd Ed.
Critical Listening and Auditory Perception
Modular Digital Multitracks: The Power User's Guide, Rev. Ed.
The Dictionary of Music Business Terms
Professional Microphone Techniques
Sound for Picture, 2nd Ed.
Music Producers, 2nd Ed.
Live Sound Reinforcement

Printed in Auburn Hills, MI
ISBN 0-87288-740-5

Contents

Acknowledgments

Craig Anderton for his invaluable expertise, Jimmy Fritz, for sharing his wealth of knowledge and *Rave Culture (An Insiders Overview)*. Please buy his book, and visit his website at **http://members.home.net/smallfryenterprises/rave/**. James and Kelly Lumb for their help and friendship, James and Virginia Fry for providing my son too many pillows for so long, Jasonic at Metavibes for the best information about dance culture on the Web **(www.metavibes.com)** The Synthesizer Museum for their incredible equipment resource **(www.synthmuseum.com)**; the same goes for the Drum Machine Museum in San Francisco **(www.drummachine.com)**. Nick McGeachin for his undying enthusiasm, Trent Warlow for the great photos, Mike Lawson for blind faith, John Pledger for being the Intertec cowboy, Joanne Zola for her part in making this a reality. Jamie Drouin, Flat Eric, Damon Langlois, Rick Erickson, Steve Stoll, Zane Vella, the BetaLounge, John Digweed, Chris Cowie, Dave Jurman, Dave Ralph, Paul Oakenfold, Johnny Vicious, Derrick Perkins, Full Sail, Rob Hoffman, Mom and Dad, Savannah, Paxton, Jazz (my dog)—sorry about the walks—and, of course, MixBooks, you guys rock!

Preface

When I began to think about writing this book, it occurred to me that the knowledge I have acquired about Remix and electronic music has taken place in a relatively few short years. When I started in the music business some 20-odd years ago, educating myself about music, equipment, and techniques came slowly. I remember the feeling of awe as I unpacked my new Korg M1 and entered into the strange and wonderful world of new sounds, sequencing, and digital information. Suddenly, there was an entirely new way of creating music that was somewhere between a piano and a rocket ship. What I discovered in the process was mostly by trial and error and learning from my mistakes.

In today's world, the tools available and new ways of learning have had a profound effect on the way that we are creating music and on the music itself. New technology has made music accessible to just about anyone. It is no longer mandatory to spend half of your childhood locked in a bedroom practicing scales. Using a computer and the right software, most of us can learn to create some form of music in a relatively short period of time. Interestingly, a parallel exists between the kid from a few years back playing his first electric guitar and kids of today starting out with computer MP3 files or two inexpensive turntables and a crossfading mixer. In both scenarios, the process and passion devoted to the art is quite similar and, despite new technology, remains a very human process. At the end of the day, it's all about creative expression, regardless of the medium.

Needless to say, technology has had a momentous effect on all facets of our society. The very way that we learn, accumulate information, and experience our muse has taken a radical shift. In this era of instant gratification, a new mentality has emerged that says it's okay to borrow from the past, present, or future, and it is also okay to recycle and mutate existing works into something new. It's a new form of expression. Using readymade or assembled samples as musical idioms, remixing has developed into the art of piecing together a musical collage. Selecting bits and bites from existing works of music combined with alternate or new ideas, remixing has developed into a dominant new production force that allows multiple variations on a theme.

The roots of electronic music are many and reach back as early as the late 1800s. Pioneers such as Homer Dudley, a Bell Lab engineer who invented the Voder in 1940 (later known as the Vocoder), developed an electronic device that was capable of synthesizing the human voice. The first Theremin, named after the Russian engineer Levon Termen, was built in 1917. The Theremin created a strange, distinctive, electronic but still musical sound.

The most profound changes have occurred in recent years. Wasn't it just yesterday that milestone products such as the Yamaha DX7 synthesizer, the Roland TB303 bass line, and the TR808 drum synthesizer found their ways to unsuspecting music stores and into the hands of early adapter musicians? Suddenly, you could find electronic keyboards, drum machines, and crude sequencers in almost every corner of the earth, used in almost every style of music.

Early giants of electronic music, such as Kraftwerk, Tangerine Dream, and Cybotron, took crude electronic instruments to their maximum potential. These innovators spawned an entirely new generation of producers who today are actively taking their music to new heights. As computers gained the ability to control digital instruments via the communication protocol called MIDI (Musical Instrument Digital Interface), progress moved swiftly. Now seemingly commonplace, almost every home computer has the capability of generating some form of electronic music. It has been said the invention of the electronic instrument is arguably the most significant musical invention of the twentieth century.

Over the past ten years, the sheer mass accessibility of computers, affordable digital instruments, and software has given rise to a worldwide proliferation of a new music and culture known as Electronica.

For me, a more in-depth knowledge of remixing and DJ culture began at the 1998 Winter NAMM Show in Los Angeles, California. As a musician, producer, and songwriter, I have spent many years developing my skills in various home and professional studios. These experiences ultimately led me to a position working in the marketing and product development department for IVL Technologies in Victoria, Canada. IVL is a DSP (digital signal processing) developer and manufacturer who has designed and built many innovative products over the years such as the DigiTech Whammy Pedal, the Studio Vocalist, Studio

5000, and recently, the DigiTech Talker. These products, along with others, also led to IVL's collaboration on such diverse products as the Mackie Digital 8 Buss and the Intonater for TC Electronics.

My interest in the world of Electronica and remixing actually came about through my involvement in the development of the DigiTech Talker. The Talker was originally designed as a guitar-oriented vocoder pedal that could electronically simulate the classic talk boxes made famous by artists such as Peter Frampton, Joe Walsh, and others.

During the marketing phase of the Talker, we discovered that the product had become popular with DJs and electronic bands, particularly in the U.K. Armed with this knowledge, we took a very close look at what was going on at the DJ booths during the next Winter NAMM show. After seeing the high level of excitement generated by these manufacturers, it was determined that there was indeed a new and growing market. IVL possessed the ideas and the technologies that could provide this market with innovative new products. With the idea of developing an exciting new product line, a great deal of time was spent consulting with DJs and remixers. This ultimately led to the standalone product line known as Electrix. With a hands-on philosophy, Electrix set out to create intuitive and easy-to-use products designed especially for remixers, DJs, musicians, and studios of all sizes.

Remix: The Electronic Music Explosion intends to provide a global look at this rapidly growing segment of the music industry. With practical explanations of what actually happens in a Remix, along with featured tools of the trade, this book will explore the roots and origins of the style, trends, and culture, along with a look at where electronic music is headed. Additionally, we provide suggestions on how to get started in the business and interviews with established artists, top producers, and record companies who specialize in the genre. *Remix* will also highlight subjects such as equipment required, how to release your own material, and how to promote yourself. The Internet has an intricate relationship with this mass underground market, and we will therefore take an in-depth look at underground radio, Electronica websites, the proliferation of MP3 files, and electronic promotion.

In this book, I use the term *Remix* in its broadest sense, as often the lines are blurred and terms have more than one meaning. Much more than a technical production term, *Remix* embraces the entire DJ culture, the lifestyle of dance music, and what has come to be known as Electronica.

Foreword

From *Rave Culture (An Insider's View)* by Jimi Fritz

Electronic dance music is not just about creating new sounds; it is about learning to listen to music in a different way. Popular music has long been dedicated to the form of the song, where a familiar musical structure of verse and chorus is remembered and recognized by the listener. The lyrics tell us what the song is about, conveying the point of view of the singer, and the music sets the mood and dictates how we should react to the content. In this way, popular songs are very much an extension of our storytelling traditions, designed to give information, share experiences, teach lessons, entertain, and so forth. Like stories, song structure has a beginning, middle, and end, a structure which also serves to help interpret and shape the material to impart its intended meaning. Songs are neatly formatted into three- or four-minute sound packages that make them easy to listen to and, more importantly, easier to showcase and sell on commercial venues such as radio and television.

Electronic dance music challenges us to develop new listening skills. With a conventional song, we listen to the form and follow the lyrics, but with electronic forms there is no beginning or end. The music is cyclic and continuous and acts more as a catalyst for our own personal musical journey, more a transportation system than an end in itself. Electronic dance music is specifically designed to make you move your body. Whether it be swaying back and forth to your internal groove, or thrashing around like a demented gymnast, the intended effect is to inspire a physical reaction. When we allow the music to influence our movements, it becomes a truly interactive adventure.

The experience of listening to electronic dance music is closer to the experience that a musician has when creating music, in that it requires a certain level of concentration and focus. In this focused state, the listener becomes closer to being a part of the musical process rather than a passive audience. The music creates a three dimensional sound environment that we both react to and interact with. Our journey is not guided by the personality or agenda of the musicians but is self-directed and, therefore, provides a more personal perspective, and one that can ultimately be more meaningful. With conventional popular music, we identify with the singer or musician, and their personalities become the focus. Electronica, on the other hand, is not as concerned with the personalities of the musicians or singers and fosters more of an egoless approach to the music.

The new sounds that are being produced by the next generation of electronic technology can be truly awe-inspiring, producing emotional effects that we are only just beginning to understand. We have long known that the vibrations caused by soundwaves can have a profound effect on our mental and emotional states. Recent developments in modern medicine are now employing soundwaves to knit together tissue and bone. It is certain that as our knowledge grows in this area, we will be using the vibrating qualities of soundwaves in the not too distant future for a variety of applications. Electronic musicians are already experimenting with subsonic and ultrasonic sounds beyond our normal hearing range. These frequencies can vibrate through our bodies without being heard and may be partly responsible for the powerful emotional response that people have when listening to electronic music. That deep bass sound that seems to penetrate and reverberate deep within your core may be giving your heart a massage while stimulating some primitive genetic memory.

The repetitive nature of electronic dance music is deceptively simple. Like the shaman's drum, it represents a symbolic beating heart, the first sound that we hear from inside the womb and one that confirms our very existence. The continual beat forces us to attune to our own rhythm and mood, acting as a bridge that connects us to ourselves, and indirectly, to each other. When played at high volume, the music demands our whole attention, becoming an audio environment that supersedes any other stimulus. In this way, it provides a context for a personal journey that can take us anywhere we want to go.

Finally, electronic dance music is not about entertainment or information. It harbors no ambition to become Number 1 in the pop charts, win prizes, or go platinum. It is not about musicians becoming stars or influencing a mass audience with a particular philosophy, opinion, or viewpoint. And it does not strive for money or power or status or any of the other goals and ambitions of most contemporary popular music.

Electronica is about a new and bright future. It is about spontaneity and change, emancipation and revolution, personal exploration and freedom. Unlike the egocentric, pain-filled, opinionated voices of pop culture, it is optimistic and enthusiastic about the future. The music does not seek to influence or manipulate but simply strives to create a musical environment designed to expand the mind, open the heart, and inspire the soul. More a transportation system than a final destination, electronic dance music is concerned with creating a musical momentum or journey. Where that journey leads is entirely up to the listener and, for those with open minds, open hearts, and a sense of adventure, the rewards can be enormous.

Evolution

IN THE BEGINNING

Remix is about dancing, creating music that leaves you with no other choice but to move. There's something about the beat that seems to grab hold of you and won't let go.

Dancing has always been music's counterpart; it's how we interact with music to create our own energy. Tribal dances were ancient culture's link to spirituality. Flappers going through the Charleston steps were the rage in the '20s, and the Jive was an essential part of the big band craze in the '30s and '40s. The '50s ushered in the Twist, the Mashed Potato, and sock hops. The early '60s found its own identity with dances such as the Swim, the Jerk, and the Watusi.

The late '60s featured an explosion of creativity coupled with huge political and cultural changes. This had a great effect on how we interacted with music. Although we still danced, there was much more focus on the content and the meaning of the music and less on a particular dance craze. For a while we primarily listened to music, knew the lyrics, went to the concerts, and strongly identified with it as a voice within us. We were serious about the music from the '60s, but in many ways, we lost the physical connection to the music.

Interestingly, in a parallel universe to the '60s counter-culture music, there was a proliferation of R&B. Motown churned out hit after hit, and areas such as Philadelphia and Detroit maintained a strong connection to rhythm-based music. It's not surprising that the seeds of disco were sewn in the same areas that had never lost their affiliation with dance music. By the early '70s, it seemed that that we suddenly developed a collective desire to rediscover dancing, have fun, and take our music less seriously. Quite possibly, the movie *Saturday Night Fever* heralded the official rebirth of popular dancing. During this time, rap and hip-hop began to develop, although they didn't reach the mainstream until much later.

Then somewhere in the early '80s, disco died, or so it seemed. In reality, the music went underground. Popular music went on to the next phase with the emergence of punk rock and new wave, followed by a trend toward a heavier rock sound which brought in new pop songs with gutsy power chords. Heavy metal and power pop flourished and paved the way for grunge in the early '90s. Then, alternative music marked the retreat to a more acoustic sound along with an increased interest in female singers.

In the mid-'80s, when hip-hop and electronic rhythms found their way into the pop charts, they were soon followed by MCs such as Run DMC, who combined many elements of modern R&B with heavy guitars and their infectious rhyming style. Soon the MCs evolved into harder-edged rappers, who spoke the language of the street and brought the hip-hop culture to the forefront. Meanwhile, disco flourished primarily in underground gay discos where it began to develop a harder rhythmic edge. This music ultimately mutated into what we now know as house. By most accounts, house derived its name from a nightclub in Chicago where Grammy-winning DJ and remixer Frankie Knuckles held nightly court for a period of five or six years. Other similar hotbeds such as the Paradise Garage and the Fun House in New York provided nightly doses of Larry Levan, John "Jellybean" Benitez, and others who inspired an entirely new generation of DJs.

Like-minded DJs in the U.K. and Germany discovered these early pioneering house DJs and emulated the sound while adding their own influences. Kraftwerk, the innovative German techno-pop group, experimented with electronic sounds in the early '70s and had a profound influence on many aspects of modern dance culture.

Just as in the '60s the Beatles and Stones reinvented their own versions of U.S. R&B, U.K. DJs such as Paul Oakenfold reinvented the driving house sound by adding their own musical influences. Soon, underground clubs and parties developed in England and Germany where masses of followers found their way to these events by word of mouth.

These parties, also known as raves, were often illegal, having no license or official authorization. Raves were secret and held in out-of-the-way warehouses and outdoor locations. The underground nature of these events added to the excitement and the growing movement. Soon, legitimate nightclubs began to spring up everywhere and a new culture was born.

The new dance movement flourished in the U.K. and Europe and grew into the largest underground music scene the world has ever known. Like a second British invasion, U.K. promoters and DJs began to export their movement back into North America, where the same phenomenon was beginning to occur.

Despite the absence of dance-oriented radio in the U.S. and Canada, by the late '90s dance culture had developed into a massive underground movement in North America. It was primarily promoted by word of mouth, flyers, and the Internet. More recently, this underground dance movement has found acceptance in popular music, as producers adopt the driving beats and other production techniques from it into mainstream music.

THE RISE OF THE DJ

Musicians who played in club bands during the early '70s learned to accept the house DJ as the one who kept the beat going when they finished a set. Dance floors were often more crowded on the breaks than when the band played. A band playing a club regularly would get to know the DJ and learn to understand the golden night club rule: *never stop the beat from pulsating for less than 20 seconds, or you'll lose the crowd.* After all, the dance floor is like an ancient ritual ground where you can meet members of the opposite sex (or of the same sex if that's your thing). By the time disco fever hit in the '70s, live gigs were becoming scarce. To understand the world of Remix, DJs, and modern dance music, it's important to learn something about its origins and its culture.

The Radio DJ

The oldest form of DJ is the radio disc jockey. Before radio formats became tightly formatted, a good radio jock might have a knack for picking up a hot new tune or, in some cases, discovering talent. With a friendly voice and a quick wit, a jock from a large market station was very influential in making or breaking a record. The '50s were rife with scandal as record companies tried to gain the favor of DJs and payola became commonplace.

The Mobile DJ

The early '70s found some DJs making a lucrative living from performing at weddings, bar mitzvahs, school dances, and office parties. A mobile DJ needs an extremely wide variety of music to satisfy the musical tastes of different groups of dancers. With crowds varying in age from 18 to 80, the mobile jock needs to be prepared to supply music from the '30s and '40s right through to the popular music of any given era. A good mobile jock has a strong instinct that keeps the dance floors filled and plays everything from "In The Mood" to "Old Time Rock and Roll" to the Chemical Brothers and a little of the Chicken dance thrown in for good measure. A good mobile DJ has an uncanny sense of music, and the better ones can earn a very good living.

The Club DJ

The pressure of maintaining a residency as a club DJ can be daunting; a club's income is more or less dependent on a particular DJ's ability to attract a packed house. A resident DJ usually has a certain style that seems to tune in to the crowd, starting with just the right mood and building to a frenzy. Although many legendary DJs work in world-famous nightclubs, they represent a very small percentage of working turntablists.

DJs often choose to promote one night a week on which they hope to attract enough customers to pay themselves. For this reason, many name their particular night to help conjure an image and create appeal. DJs specialize in certain styles of music and, if they are successful, the club is full and everyone's happy. However, the stability factor of DJs is not extremely high due to rapidly changing tastes and crowds that are fickle. What is trendy one week may be next week's old hat.

The Rave DJ

The most recent addition to the DJ family is the Rave DJ. The mandate for this style of music is to take the listener on a nonstop journey filled with highs and lows and fast and slow moments. Although other substances may play a role in shows, most raves are usually nonalcohol events that tend to cater to a somewhat younger crowd. Picture the Moontribe events held in the desert outside of Los Angles on the full moon. Imagine a great DJ playing your favorite type of music through a large sound system while the sun rises…it's a spectacular—almost spiritual—moment in time.

Many DJs are augmenting their acts with a variety of digital electronic instruments.

Often known as *live PA,* this style of DJing relies on musical dance sense combined with the technical ability to control MIDI gear, synthesizers, and signal processors. Many bands are beginning to incorporate DJs into the traditional drums, guitar, and bass format.

Fig. #1: DJ

ORIGINS OF REMIX

The term Remix first surfaced around the early '80s, although few understood the concept back then. One example of remixing is when Madonna took the preproduction versions of her recordings to popular DJs at popular New York dance clubs for feedback and suggestions. What better place to anonymously test a song's dance potential? Although considered a pop artist, Madonna's music has always been very rhythmic and dance-oriented, and much of her success is due to her huge dance club following. Madonna and other artists realized the value of a DJ's intuitive knowledge of what makes people want to dance. Soon, artists and record companies were taking the DJ quite seriously.

Many of today's top DJs and Remix artists got their start as mobile and club DJs. With a good knowledge of music, the right sound systems, and a winning dance formula, a top DJ can attract the interest of producers, artists, and record labels. Musicians, recording engineers, and producers also realized the usefulness of people with dance floor savvy. It was perhaps at this early junction that the DJ and the musician began to merge. Many remixers of today have backgrounds in both worlds.

Today, Remix has evolved to where the producer/remixer will often actually replace all the existing tracks with new material. A remixer might be supplied with only the lead vocal on a DAT tape; it then becomes the remixer's job to rebuild the music from the ground up. This is not considered a replacement of the original recording, but rather an alternate version that could give the song more dance floor potential.

The music heard in dance clubs around the world is considerably different than the versions played on popular radio stations. The origins of this are when dance-oriented radio songs of the '70s began to include *extended mixes* for the dance floor. Nightclubs needed more time to create a groove that would get people dancing than the three- or four-minute radio cuts would allow. DJs instinctively know that you have allow enough time for people to recognize their favorite songs, get up the nerve to ask a partner to dance, hit the dance floor, and get into the rhythm. After all this, club goers don't want the experience to be over in a few short minutes, especially if they're interested in pursuing their partners further.

The Early Days

Smart record producers from the early '70s realized that they could create radio cuts and extended mixes of the same song. These extended plays were actually early *remixes*, better known as *club mixes*.

Pioneers of dance production realized there was a huge sonic difference between a typical 45 rpm single that was destined for radio play and what would sound good through a large, high volume club system. Generally, 45s accented midrange frequencies because heavy bass sounds do not translate well to radio. Remixers tweaked a song's tonal balance to create a separate mix that fully exploited the fidelity of a dance club's sound system.

Early methods of extending songs included manually splicing the master tape or mixing live onto a new master. A good mixer would create an extended mix version of a release by adding drum breaks, adjusting volumes, and accentuating certain sections to create a longer version of the original. Using various techniques such as sound-on-sound tape decks and DJ mixers, two copies of the same record can be dubbed together by cross-fading separate sources to expand a cuts' time (for example, you can fade in the beginning of a break from one source as the other source's break is ending). Frequencies and volumes were adjusted at the same time to create a dance club mix.

Live DJs developed the ability to extend a mix of a song on-the-fly using beat-matching skills. Using headphones to cue an upcoming record, one piece of music can segue into another by slightly adjusting a turntable's speed or pitch control to match tempos. Once the tempos are matched, the DJ is able to cross-fade or switch from one turntable (or other sound source) to another, while maintaining a constant beat. DJs hone this skill and develop their own reputations for a particular style of music and for their ability to create a live extended mix. There's a lot more to being a good DJ than simply selecting music and spinning another record.

In 1973, Technics introduced the SL-1200 turntable to the market (Fig. #2). The durability and features of this turntable made it the standard of the DJ industry. With its direct-drive, strobe-monitored platter, the near-mythical SL-1200MK2 "Wheel of Steel" (as many call it) gave DJs the only motor capable of withstanding high torque starts and record gripping stops. This was required by a DJ's "scratch" moves, where the DJ plays the record like a musical instrument, starting, stopping, and moving the record manually (we'll talk more about scratching later). In many ways, this turntable provided the fuel for the Remix movement, just as the electric guitar paved the way for rock music several decades earlier.

Fig. #2: Technics SL-1200 turntable

To cater to the DJ, record companies started to break with the tradition of seven-inch, 45 rpm records that were usually two or three minutes in length. The first seven-inch extended mix single appeared in the U.S. in 1974 as a promotional single. But very few seven-inch extended mix titles were commercially successful, as the sound quality of the these singles was limited by the medium itself. Louder grooves took up more space, so to fit more time on a single you had to turn down the music's level to compensate. This made surface noise and other imperfections associated with vinyl more obvious.

The 12-inch single was then developed so that DJs could create longer dance versions of a radio hit. In 1975, a few select DJs convinced several small record labels and recording engineers to make up test pressings of select mixes on 12-inch vinyl to achieve superior audio fidelity. These promotional only "white label" pressings became popular with DJs and fans who wanted the club version of a release.

DJs discovered a great demand for nonstop extended dance mixes. Eight-track and cassette tape bootlegs soon began to appear. Frustrated, record companies countered by releasing extended mix compilation LPs that simulated a night at a dance club. These special releases came out after a song had already peaked and was on its way down the charts. Extended plays were a great way for the record companies to achieve additional sales from a given title.

In 1976, Salsoul Records of New York conceived the idea of pressing special 12-inch releases of their new artists (Fig. #3). They began to distribute these releases to record stores around the country at a list price of $2.98. Initially skeptical, record stores soon found that there was a blossoming new market for these new big singles that were at first thought to be overpriced. It was then that modern dance music truly came into its own.

Fig. #3: Salsoul Records, 12-inch "Giant Single"

The major record labels originally thought the limited edition 12-inch release would help sell the LP, but the 12-inch version often outsold the original recording. This realization forced record companies to limit their 12-inch releases for fear of cannibalizing the original LP. As a result, many of the most coveted titles prior to 1983 were released as promotional only pressings that featured "extended mixes" for radio station and nightclub use only.

TOM MOULTON[1]

Many seven-inch singles in the early '70s averaged a mere three minutes in length, hardly enough time for patrons to get out of their chairs and hit the dance floor. Then a few DJs created longer mixes by cross-fading two seven-inch singles of the same song together "live" on their turntables; as one single was faded out, the other would be faded in right on the beat to create a longer mix. One notable DJ in this pioneering mixing innovation was Tom Moulton. Many collectors may know his name from the hundreds of great disco mixes he produced on seven-inch singles in the '75-76 era that boasted of being a Tom Moulton Mix.

Tom Moulton was a fashion model on hiatus from the music business when he visited Fire Island's Hotel during a photo shoot. He said, "I got a charge out of it, all these white people dancing to black music." Painstakingly, he spent 80 hours making a 90-minute dance tape using sound-on-sound and varispeed (to tweak the tempo for beat-matching), and created a nonstop musical event. The hotel's owner rejected the tape, but the competing Sandpiper club offered to listen and Moulton left the reel. At 2:30 on a Saturday morning, Moulton was awakened by a call from the Sandpiper that was unintelligible except for the screaming of dancers dancing to a tape!

Moulton worked in promotion for Scepter Records and mixed DCA Productions' "Dream World" by Don Downing for the label. In 1974, when DCA called him to work on Gloria Gaynor's first album, he made history. "Never Can Say Goodbye" was a medley of three long songs, segued together to create an entire LP side. Meco Monardo said it was "a revelation" when Moulton extended three-minute songs to more than six by lengthening the instrumental section. But Moulton also knew that this would intensify and modulate the impact of a song or a series of songs. Incredibly, Moulton's credit did not appear on the album because of a potential conflict; he had launched the first music trade-paper column on the scene, "Disco Mix," in *Billboard*.

Tom Moulton's concepts single-handedly created a new industry of remixing; the art of producing records with greater dance impact. By rebalancing the frequency range, he extended the high frequencies much further than Motown ever did. As Moulton noted, "Because 45s were geared for radio you couldn't cut a lot of bass onto the record. A lot of records didn't have the fidelity and sounded terrible. However, people were playing them for the songs, not for the fidelity."

Regard for the integrity of a song also guided Moulton in the studio. He not only sharpened sound for high-volume nightclub play, but he also restructured records, setting up the hooks and repeating the best parts, greatly amplifying the original song scheme's tension and release. He'd tweak levels obsessively all through the record, effectively rephrasing a track or vocal by hitting the volume control when he felt it would increase intensity. He said, "I was so wired into the song. They thought I was crazy. But you go for the blood and guts, the thing that really counts in a song." Moulton's hook might be a mistake by the players, and he points out that the insane sonic power of "Disco Inferno" happened when he was compensating for a console that was set up wrong. Repeatedly, with the simple woodblock in "More, More, More (Part 1)," in the strong but never overdone pop pump of "Instant Replay," Moulton made good records even stronger. His blueprint has been used thousands of times over.

Remix: The Electronic Music Explosion

Like everything else in disco, remixing started to become formulaic, but this wasn't Moulton's fault. He often critiqued remixers for making music into a DJ tool, instead of mixing to maximize a song's original intent. Moulton used drum breaks, for example, as transitions within a song to set up an emotional rush with the return of the rest of the music. Key changes made a break necessary to create dramatic structure; not merely because drum breaks made it easier for a DJ to mix in or out of a record.

"People have said, you make disco records, and I said, wrong, I make records you can dance to. I wouldn't know how to make a record just for discos," Moulton once said.

As the disco sound and lifestyle hit full speed in 1977, many new disco releases followed from both large and small record labels. These gave the best mixing DJs the opportunity to create a name for themselves though the special mixes they crafted that added their personal style to club hits. Notable remixers of this era were Jim Burgess, Larry Levan, Jimmy Simpson, John Luongo, David Todd, Walter Gibbons, Rick Gianatos, Richie Rivera, and of course, Tom Moulton.

Most remixers had been previously involved in the post-production phase of a single release, but the success of the Remix style caused many record labels to consult first with a remixer before actually releasing the seven-inch single or LP track. During this time, the DJ's involvement shifted from the live mixing method to the more technical in-studio remixing or splicing of the master tape. The remixer's job now not only required creative vision, but also technical ability in the studio.

33-1/3 rpm took over from 45 rpm as the standard for records to best represent the sound quality obtained in the studio. In 1976, Salsoul Records released the first album where the DJ/remixer got top billing over the original artist when Larry Levan remixed the classic "Ain't No Mountain High Enough" and added an incredible synth workout. This was originally released as a two 12-inch promo-pack in December 1978.

VINCENT MONTANA, JR.[2]

The Godfather of Disco?

Vincent Montana, Jr. (Fig. #4), a multitalented composer/ arranger/conductor and renowned vibraharpist, is responsible for countless gold and platinum albums. The Philadelphia Sound, MFSB, and the Salsoul Orchestra are among his many credits.

Born and raised in the heart of South Philadelphia, Montana was playing local dance clubs by the time he was 16. During the early '50s he worked in jazz clubs as a backup for such legends as Charlie (Bird) Parker, Sarah Vaughn, Buddy DeFranco, Stan Getz, Clifford Brown, and Red Garland. By spanning every contemporary musical style into a dance matrix, Montana's SalSoul Orchestra set a musical standard by introducing the first "Disco orchestra" to innovate a new style of dance music. Whether the record company realized it or not, the six albums Montana composed, arranged, and recorded for SalSoul changed the face of the disco era.

Fig. #4: Vincent Montana is credited with creating the "Disco Orchestra" sound.

Perhaps the most culturally influenced modern dance style, the music that we now know as hip-hop began to develop in New York City's South Bronx in the '70s. Musician KRS-ONE (Kris Parker), a recognized authority on hip-hop culture, feels that "the basic psychology of hip-hop is to express oneself first and then explain. If you try to explain what you're doing before you do it, you'll never do it. Hip-hop is sometimes taken to mean rap music, but it ought to include graffiti art, a dance style called breakin', the language, fashion, and culture of the street."

According to most, hip-hop began in New York and was influenced by interactions between African-American New Yorkers and new immigrants from China, the Caribbean, Europe, and Latin America. This multicultural mix led to the development of a new socio-economic system, starting with food, clothes, and artistic expression. From Parker's perspective, "hip-hop culture exploded in New York between 1975 and 1979. Break[dancing], bombing trains and buses with graffiti, [and] listening to DJs like Kool Herc play records by James Brown or Sly and the Family Stone became a fundamental part of New York street life."

DJ KOOL HERC

In the earliest days of hip-hop music and culture when skills were developing on the streets of the South Bronx, the DJ was the center of all entertainment. Legend has it that a Jamaican expatriate and reggae fan named DJ Kool started it all when he took the concept of the booming mobile sound system to uptown streets and recreation centers. He gave the partygoers what they wanted, hard funk beats manually spliced together to play for hours at a time. The breakers went wild, the heads of aspiring future DJs in the audience began to spin, and hip-hop was born.

By most accounts, Herc was the first DJ to buy two copies of the same record for just a 15-second break (rhythmic instrumental segment) in the middle. By mixing back and forth between the two copies, he was able to double, triple, or extend the break indefinitely. In so doing, Herc effectively deconstructed and reconstructed so-called found sound, using the turntable as a musical instrument.

Scratching

Scratching (back-spinning a record) most likely came about by accident; as the story goes, Grandwizard Theodore was practicing in his bedroom, backspinning something, when his mother told him to turn the record down. When he did this to hear what she was saying, he heard himself rubbing the record in his headphones. When she left, he kept rubbing the record because he liked the beat it created; a week later, he sprung this technique on a dance crowd.

Turntablism in the Early '80s[4]

Grandmixer D. St, (now called DXT), a member of Afrika Bambaataa's Zulu Nation, most clearly articulated the idea of the turntablist as an instrumentalist with his orchestrated scratch solo on the most influential DJ track of them all, Bill Laswell's 1983 production of Herbie Hancock's "Rockit."

"I remember listening to DJs like him take the turntable and coax all these sounds from it that you couldn't get if you just let the record play. I started thinking that this is an art that I could really get into because I already liked the music, and being able to make my own music off the records that I'm using is something that I could see myself doing."

From its inception, hip-hop was defined by an approach to sound and music-making rather than a single stylistic designation. jazz, soul, funk, rock and roll, Nigerian drumming, everything was in the mix. The parties were a cross-cultural barrage of styles chosen and mixed by the disc jockey. Jamaican-born Bronx resident DJ Kool Herc provided the innovations that elevated DJing into an art form.

The buzz surrounding hip-hop had already migrated via mixed tapes aired on boomboxes to Manhattan, but its birthplace was the South Bronx, where Afrika Bambaataa and his crew of black youth known as the Zulu Nation gathered to celebrate the new sensation.

Afrika Bambaataa[5]

A seminal Bronx DJ during the '70s, Afrika Bambaataa ascended to godfather status with "Planet Rock," the 1982 hip-hop classic which blended the beats of hip-hop with techno-pop futurism inspired by German pioneers Kraftwerk. Even before he began recording in 1980, Bambaataa was hip-hop's foremost DJ, an organizer and promoter of the large block parties during the mid to late '70s that presaged the rise of rap. After the success of "Planet Rock," he recorded electro-oriented rap only sparingly, concentrating instead on fusion, exemplified by his singles with ex-Sex Pistol John Lydon and fellow godfather James Brown. Bambaataa had moved to the background by the late '80s as far as hip-hop was concerned, but the rise of his Zulu Nation collective (including De La Soul, Queen Latifah, A Tribe Called Quest, and the Jungle Brothers) found him once more being tipped as one of rap's founding fathers.

Born Kevin Donovan in the Bronx on April 10, 1960, Afrika Bambaataa Aasim took his name from a nineteenth-century Zulu chief. Beginning in 1977, Bambaataa began organizing block parties and breakdancing competitions around the Bronx. His excellent turntable techniques led many to proclaim him the best DJ in the business (although Grandmaster Flash and DJ Kool Herc were more innovative), and his record debut as a producer came in 1980 with Soul Sonic Force's "Zulu Nation Throwdown." The single was a rallying cry for the Zulu Nation, a group of like-minded Afrocentric musicians who only gained fame in the late '80s, but who had influenced the rise of hip-hop throughout the decade.

"Jazzy Sensation," Afrika Bambaata & the Jazzy Five's groundbreaking release, was produced by Arthur Baker and Shep Pettibone in March 1981 on Tommy Boy Records.

This record is considered by many to be the first commercial hip-hop release. Bambaataa, whose influences ranged from Nigerian drumming to the Monkees to James Brown and Kraftwerk, was a true visionary who opened his ears to a plethora of styles and cultures. In the process, he created his own musical revolution.

ARTHUR BAKER

Arthur Baker first drew attention in 1982 when he discovered the multi-platinum R&B group New Edition. The following year, he received the Billboard Trendsetter Award for producing Afrika Bambaata's "Planet Rock." This was followed by a string of electro killers with the Soul Sonic Force, Rocker's Revenge classic "Walking On Sunshine," and "IOU" by Freeez.

As one of the original dance remixers (he has a DJ background), in the '80s Baker transformed such tracks as Bruce Springsteen's "Dancing in the Dark" and "Born in the U.S.A," and Cyndi Lauper's "Girls Just Want to Have Fun" into dance classics. He also co-wrote and produced New Order's classic "Confusion."

SHEP PETTIBONE[6]

Famed for his late '80s/early '90s Remix and production work for Madonna and other major-league pop stars, Pettibone's early origins lie in hip-hop. Together with Arthur Baker, he was behind Afrika Bambaata & the Jazzy Five's groundbreaking "Jazzy Sensation" release, which was actually a remake of Gwen McCrae's "Funky Sensation." He also pioneered the mastermixes of Kiss FM Radio, introducing a new methodology by segueing records to build sequences, almost like movements in classical music. Examples of this can be found on Prelude Records' *Kiss 98.7FM*.

In 1982-1983 saw Shep moving into another musical area, reviving the sounds of people like Loleatta Holloway, Rochelle Fleming, and Jocely Brown to great success, which ensured his status as an in-demand mixer for large budget studio sessions. His work with Madonna became legendary and led to his highly-in-demand remixer status.

The MC

As the music and the culture progressed, clubs and parties began to feature MCs (masters of ceremonies) who were used as props to direct attention to the DJ. They would talk to the crowd and encourage them feel the groove, dance, and enjoy themselves. Soon MCs began to speak more freely, sometimes making rhymes. Gradually the MC evolved into today's rap musician. In 1979, Sylvia Robinson founded Sugar Hill Records in Englewood, New Jersey and put out "Rapper's Delight," which is generally acknowledged as the first rap album. She got three guys together and said, "Look, say these rhymes." They called themselves the Sugar Hill Gang and "Rapper's Delight" went on to sell five million records.

A modern evolution of jazz, R&B, and soul, hip-hop is stylistically based on hybrid 12-base (shuffle rhythms), which often feature classic Roland TR-808 and TR-707 drum machines. Using samplers, keyboards, and scratching, hip-hop began to move from the streets to the mainstream. With early heavy weight adopters such as Miles Davis and Herbie Hancock, hip-hop has emerged as a dominant musical force that has found its way into numerous musical genres.

DISCO REBORN

When disco stared to decline in the late '70s, the reign of artists such as Donna Summer gave way to the likes of Michael Jackson, Van Halen, and a new generation of '80s performers. Formerly popular discos were now passé and fodder for numerous comedy skits.

As the '80s dawned, many were already writing disco's obituary. In the summer of 1979, the rock group The Knack blasted through disco's radio domination with the pounding rock of "My Sharona." In an effort to hasten disco's downfall, radio DJ Steve Dahl engineered a near riot and mass burning of disco records. For many, disco's future looked grim.

The Birth of House

If disco died, it found a North American afterlife in underground clubs and baths of the late '70s and early '80s. With a predominantly gay clientele, disco continued to fly the flag on established turf where it began to mature and mutate. Clubbers in urban centers like New York, Philadelphia, San Francisco, and Chicago continued to carry the torch for modern dance music, while the mainstream veered in new directions. Hot spots such as New York's Paradise Garage and The Loft, Chicago's Warehouse and Music Box, and San Francisco's Trocadero Transfer became incubators for the new dance culture. Musical styles that evolved even borrowed their names from the legendary clubs that bore them.

The Clubs, The Legends:
The Warehouse and The Music Box, Chicago,
1977-1983[7]

It's widely accepted that this legendary Chicago club gave house music its name. Ironically, The Warehouse's first choice for a DJ was Larry Levan, who declined. Larry stayed in New York but recommend his friend Frankie Knuckles. Between 1977 and 1983, Knuckles presided over the club, moving to Chicago from New York City in 1977. Frankie played a mixture of underground disco, funk, soul, and classic Philly sounds to a predominantly black, gay following. Like the majority of American cities of the day, Chicago was a rock and blues town with plenty of live music and beer-swilling bars, but not much in the way of dancing or clubs. Knuckles and fellow Chicago DJ Ron Hardy unwittingly changed the lives of thousands of people in the late '80s and early '90s.

From his residency at Chicago's Music Box Club, Ron Hardy created the environment for the house explosion. Where Knuckles' sound was still very much based in disco, Hardy was the DJ that went for the rawest, wildest rhythm tracks he could find. He made The Music Box the inspirational temple for almost every DJ and producer to come out of the Chicago scene.

Frankie Knuckles[8]

The man many call the godfather of house, Frankie Knuckles, began DJing in New York in the early '70s while still a teenager, years before the disco boom. Ten years later he was in Chicago, putting together megamixes of old disco hits by adding new drum-machine percussion. He had an appreciative audience at crucial clubs like the Music Box and the Warehouse. From those first formative steps came house music.

A decade later, Knuckles was back in his New York home, working as a producer and remixer for the biggest pop stars in the business. His career spans more time than any dance producer; without him the landscape would be immeasurably different.

Born in the Bronx in 1955, Knuckles listened to a lot of jazz as a child, thanks to his sister's record collection. He studied commercial art and costume design before taking his first job as a DJ in 1971. Several years later, he hooked up with childhood friend Larry Levan, and the two began working at Nicky Siano's New York club, the Gallery. Levan later moved to the Continental Baths, and Knuckles worked at another club for several months before rejoining Levan. Again, Levan left—this time to set up his own club, the Soho Place—and Knuckles continued on until the Continental Baths was closed.

The Clubs, The Legends:
The Paradise Garage, New York,
1977-1987

"The Garage, Better Days, were the clubs, that we as young, single, black women, could just go to dance and not be harassed by men. You always felt safe. These guys treated us like their baby sisters or something, totally protective…it was incredible. Much love. The best clubs were always the black gay clubs," said one club-goer of this era.

Paradise Garage, located at 84 King Street in New York, was a legendary club that operated between 1977 and 1987. The Paradise Garage club gave its name to Garage, New York's flavor of underground dance music. The Garage was Larry Levan's club, the regular DJ from the very beginning to the last night. It was a huge warehouse space that was converted from a garage into a membership-only club. It partially opened in 1977, with only the smaller room and a sound system that had been specifically designed by Larry Levan and sound designer Richard Long.

Larry Levan

Together with contemporary DJs like Tee Scott, David Mancuso, and Nicky Sianto, Larry Levan (Fig. #5) helped define house, garage and dance music in general. As a DJ, Larry has an impeccable sense of style and taste and mixed around 80 songs for over 15 labels. Many of today's most successful producers and DJs credit their first exposure to Larry's music at the Garage as a moment that changed their lives forever and inspired their whole careers. Larry had a style of playing fierce bass lines over the Garage's brilliant Richard Long–sound system.

"The sound at the Garage was unquestionably the best in any club ever and was so pure that you could carry on a conversation next to one of the huge bass speakers and not have to raise your voice. Everybody loved Larry and treated him like royalty. He was famous for making records hot and for making people sweat. I remember walking into the Garage on hot summer nights and being overcome by a heat wave of thousands of people packed on the dance floor, screaming to every new record that Larry put on and unfazed by the temperature and body jam." *(Bobbie Viteritti).*

Fig. #5: Larry Levan had a style of playing fierce bass lines over the Garage's brilliant sound system.

The Clubs, The Legends:
Trocadero Transfer, San Francisco, 1978-1981[9]

In its heyday (the late '70s/early '80s), Trocadero Transfer was regarded as the best hardcore disco club on the West Coast and one of the best in the country. There was no theme decor or fancy decoration, just a great classic disco whose fame was almost entirely due to the talent and style of DJ Bobby Viteritti and light man Billy Langenheim (remembered by many as one of the best DJ booth partnerships ever). Everything about these guys was pro, and a broad circle of club people admired them across the country. A loyal family of regulars knew what was going on through every mix and treated Trocadero like it was a religion.

Troc was a place where every night was special and the standards of music, lighting, and partying were constantly being elevated to new heights. Bad mixes were rare, and the synergy of light and sound during a mix was pure magic. Viteritti and Langeheim formed a tight team that was creative, consistent, and hard working, and the result is their legend and the influence they had on tens of thousands of people who partied at Trocadero.

Trocadero was the type of club where the art of partying was taken very seriously; pop hits and bright lights had no role there, and outsiders were scrutinized before they were welcome in its semi-private world of weekend ritual, drugs, and music.

Like most of the gay drug clubs of the era, Trocadero was a protected world with few rules except that the music and lights be brilliant and that the Saturday nights blend into Sunday mornings with a memorable sense of style.

Bobbie Viteritti. Billboard National DJ of the Year, 1979 and 1980

Bobby Viteritti's (Fig. #6) genius was in his ability to build a mood on a dance floor and to keep you dancing all night long through mixes of unbelievable energy—or unbelievable disorientation, which was a state that most of us were in while he was playing. He was famous for leaving a record—momentarily—by mixing into a perfectly matched instrumental passage in another song—and then back into the original record at a different place—and then out to his own personal version (tape edit) of another song. The effect was a brilliant combination of entertainment, amazement, and vertigo, because just when you figured out where you were, you'd get lost again.

In this day and age with quartz-locked turntables, drum machine-produced records, sampling devices, CD mixers, and digital tricks, DJs can pull off stunts like that easily, but back then it wasn't so easy.

Fig. #6: Armed only with instinct, experience, and talent, Bobby Viteritti was a master DJ in the era of belt-driven turntables and hand-cut tape edits

From the earliest incarnations of electronic music, writers and producers have been mesmerized by unusual electronic sounds. Pioneers like John Cage, Pierre Schaeffer, and Pierre Henry all experimented with the so-called found sound, combining recordings of real-life sounds into traditional composition. Karl-heinz Stockhausen gave concerts by running recordings through layers of early hand-built effects. Steve Reich experimented with pitch manipulation using varying tape speeds and tape splicing to combine one piece of music with another. This became the primary method of manipulating sound until the invention of the digital sampler in the early '80s. When Bob Moog introduced the Moog synthesizer, Wendy Carlos created a sensation by using it as the primary instrument on her wildly successful "Switched On Bach." This recording undoubtedly led to popularity of the Moog in rock music. Soon groups like Emerson, Lake, and Palmer, Tangerine Dream, the Beatles, and Kraftwerk incorporated these fascinating new sounds into their music.

Techno[10]

If there is one central idea in techno, it is of the harmony between man and machine. As Juan Atkins puts it, "You gotta look at it like techno is technological. It's an attitude to making music that sounds futuristic: something that hasn't been done before."

Techno, using the 4/4 beat structure of house combined with purely electronic sounds, seems to have its beginnings in an unlikely location: Detroit. In 1981, Juan Atkins and Rick Davis formed Cybotron, fusing austere European techno-pop with street-level funk. Predominantly built on percussive tracks, these early techno sounds were largely influenced by the German techno-pop group Kraftwerk and a series of electronic tracks from the Italo label in Italy.

In 1985, Atkins formed Metroplex Records but had no idea of the amount of worldwide impact his music would inspire. Prior to this period, almost all dance music had been based on real recordings of actual musicians. Although there have been pioneers in electronic music since the late 1800s, techno is probably the first musical genre to totally embrace machines while gaining acceptance with a large base of listeners. Quite likely, the emergence of techno in the late twentieth century may represent the unofficial and perhaps subliminal cultural acceptance of the digital age.

Kraftwerk[11]

Kraftwerk (Fig. #7) stands at the junction between the old European avant-garde and today's Euro-American pop culture. Like many others of their generation, Florian Schneider and Ralf Hütter were presented with a blank slate in postwar Germany. As Hütter explains, "When we started, it was like shock, silence. Where do we stand? Nothing. We had no father figures, no continuous tradition of entertainment. Through the '50s and '60s, everything was Americanized, directed toward consumer behavior. We were part of this 1968 movement, where suddenly there were possibilities, then we started to establish some form of German industrial sound."

Fig. #7: Kraftwerk were true pioneers of the Futuristic sound.

Classically trained, Hütter and Schneider avoided the excesses of their contemporaries, along with the guitar/bass/drums format. Their early records are full of long, moody electronic pieces, using noise and industrial elements—music being indivisible from everyday sounds. They demonstrated a strong sense of presentation (the group logo for their first three records was a traffic cone). This was part of a general move toward control over every aspect of the music and image-making process. In 1973-74, the group built their own studio in Düsseldorf, Kling Klang.

At the same time, Kraftwerk bought a Moog synthesizer. The first fruit of this was "Autobahn," a 22-minute motorway journey, from the noises of a car starting up to the hum of cooling machinery. In 1975, an edited version of "Autobahn" was a Top 10 hit.

The breakthrough came with 1977's Trans-Europe Express—again, the concentration on speed, travel, pan-Europeanism. The album's center is the 13-minute sequence that simulates a rail journey: the click-clack of metal wheels on metal rails, the rise and fade of a whistle as the train passes, the creaking of coach bodies, the final screech of metal on metal as the train stops. If this wasn't astounding enough, 1978's *The Man Machine* further developed ideas of an international language, of the synthesis between man and machine.

"The 'soul' of the machines has always been a part of our music. Trance always belongs to repetition, and everybody is looking for trance in life...in sex, in the emotional, in pleasure, in anything...so, the machines produce an absolutely perfect trance." —Ralf Hütter, 1991, quoted in Kraftwerk: *Man Machine and Music*, by Pascal Bussy.

RAVE—THE NEW BRITISH INVASION

"Let's get this straight: the story of British youth culture since the end of World War II has been the story of working class dance culture. From the post-war days of the Jitterbug, demob suits, big bands and ballrooms with names like the Locarno and Mecca through the Teddy boys bopping to Bill Haley, amphetamine-fuelled Mods out on the floor every weekend dancing to early Motown and R&B through the Northern soul and Southern Funk scenes of the '70s and to the warehouse parties of the '80s and raves of this decade, dance music has been a focal point of working-class youth culture.

"Maybe it was only when former public schoolboys found that they could make fortunes from promoting raves, and reporters fresh out of university—Jesus and Mary Chain albums tucked under their arms—realized that dance music and E [the drug ecstasy] were hot media stories, did dance music usurp rock as the fashionable lifestyle soundtrack amongst the middle class," wrote Jay Strongman in the U.K. magazine *Vibe*.

It's been said that dance culture in the U.K. *is* youth culture. With the proliferation of dance radio, nightclubs, magazines, and fashion, dance culture has systematically done the unthinkable: it has overshadowed rock and roll. Turntables now outsell the electric guitar by a margin of three to one. But how did all of this happen? How did the DJs achieve rock star status? The answer is simple: accessibility.

Kids of the dance culture generation grew up in an instant gratification world. Computers, video games, cellular phones, and television assured that this generation has been raised on technology. Is it any wonder that they embrace electronic music as their own? It's no doubt far less time-consuming and a quicker reward to become a bedroom DJ than to learn play a musical instrument well. Not only that, their electronic-based music is more likely to be played on a computer that on a guitar. This, coupled with the return of dancing as a tribal-like way to interact with music, completes the cultural loop.

Additionally, the dance world is thought to be somewhat subversive and underground, similar to rock and roll in its infancy. Can this do anything but fuel excitement? Raves bypass the local authorities that may decide to shut down operations at any given moment. Internet sites and small event flyers (with a phone number for last minute directions) serve to generate a feeling of daring and excitement. The old rallying cry of "sex, drugs and rock and roll" has been replaced with "dance and sex and drugs and dance, dance, dance."

North America is the next target. Dance culture, also known by the record company term Electronica, is now a new force in society. Raves and dance clubs are finding acceptance in even the most remote areas. Again, the underground nature of this lifestyle serves to make it even more exciting. But who are some of the architects of the new U.K. dance culture?

Paul Oakenfold

A giant in the world of electronic dance music, Paul Oakenfold began his early career as a hip-hop promoter and agent for the likes of the Beastie Boys and RunDMC. Oakenfold was there at the very beginning when itinerant Brits began staging all-night dance parties at Ibiza, a Mediterranean island off Spain, which was known for its easy pace and relaxed atmosphere. As a playground for the rich, it is likely that Ibiza afforded a very liberal setting for these early parties, and it remains to this day as the Mecca for electronic dance culture.

Oakenfold was one of the first promoters to bring this new cultural phenomenon back to England. In 1985, Oakenfold opened the first rave club in England, the Fun House, (later known as the Project Club and the Future). It was here that the emerging electronic dance movement was first introduced to English music fans eager for something new and exciting. This in turn led to the birth of acid house in the U.K. and eventually to the global rave movement.

Ibiza, Spain

By the '60s, Ibiza (Fig. #8) had attained worldwide fame as a haven for hippies and artists. In the '70s, the international jet set discovered this charming island for themselves, staging legendary parties there. Today, it seems that the international techno/house scene has chosen Ibiza as the party capital of the world. However, what many do not know is that Ibiza is not just a wild party island—it inspires above all with its stunning natural beauty. It lies like a jewel in the Mediterranean with its white beaches, azure-blue waters, rich green pine forests, and the rusty-red earth of the island.

Fig. #8: Ibiza Spain, the techno/house party capital of the world

Something Old, Something New, Something Borrowed

Like the never-ending division of human cells, electronic dance music has progressed and mutated into a seemingly endless variety of subgenres. Constantly reinventing itself, this music seems to unabashedly borrow from the present and the past by using samples (digital recordings) by everyone from James Brown to Joni Mitchell. Until recently, the unauthorized sampling of previous works ran rampant, as the laws were not as up to date as the technology.

For a while, when we heard the signature James Brown "I feel good" dropped into the middle of a piece of unrelated music, it was probably safe to say that he was not getting any royalties, as there was no law that addressed this new phenomenon. Thankfully, publishers moved quickly to correct this situation by updating the laws. Now when any copyrighted piece of music appears in a remix or as a sample in an unrelated record, the writer will receive credit and royalties.

Remix: The Electronic Music Explosion

In an unexpected way, electronic music actually pays homage to music and serves as an archive that can expose an entirely new generation to a classic piece of music. Don't forget this is a "cut and paste" generation, and the idea of recycling a piece of music is not that hard to imagine. To a dance crowd, the difference between a new rhythm and an existing one becomes meaningless, as long as it gets people on the dance floor.

Electronic music in all likelihood is *not* a fad. It simply has too many fronts and too much history to go away anytime soon. Just as the early '50s gave us rock and roll, which splintered into numerous subgenres (acid, folk, progressive, punk, country rock, etc.), electronic music has found its way to a new generation of youth who are attracted to not only its music but its culture. Thirty years from now we may well look back at the history of electronica and realize that indeed, it was here to stay.

IN THE WORDS OF A DJ

Interview with Brent Carmichael

Brent Carmichael (Fig. #9) is a veteran west coast DJ with Phatt Phunk Records out of Los Angeles, and the resident DJ at Storm in Victoria, Canada. Storm is well known as one of the best night clubs around and also serves as a showcase for local DJs and visiting luminaries from all over the world.

Fig. #9: Brent Carmichael

Brent has been spinning vinyl for several decades and has seen many musical genres come and go. From disco to new wave to house, Brent has adapted to the changing times, maintaining a well-deserved reputation for excellence throughout.—*Jimmy Fritz*

JF: When I first heard that house music evolved from disco, I had a hard time reconciling the two. How did we get from the commercial sounds of disco to the underground sound of house?

BC: Disco and house are almost the same thing. Seventies disco has a few more vocals, but it's basically house music. When people think of disco, they think of '80s disco, but just like now you can get pop-techno or pop-house, you had pop-disco. Disco was one of the first musical forms that separated it from live instruments. It always had those long instrumental eight-bar phrases, like house music today. All the house and techno music today came directly from '70s disco.

JF: How would you describe house music now?

BC: House is a culturally based music rather than industry-based, so it has geographical centers. New York house has real instruments and vocal choruses, Detroit house is much more electronic, and it's really Detroit techno. Chicago house has that galloping rhythm most people associate with house music today.

JF: What's the relationship between house and techno?

BC: To trace the musical evolution, you have to hear the music in a certain time period. If you listen to Inner City, who helped to pioneer the Detroit techno sound, you might think that it sounds like disco, but the instrumentation is different. The original techno wasn't meant to be something heavy and fast or dark and evil, it was a very musically correct form. It's only much later that it reanimated as a darker form. Stacy Pullen, who is the new school of Detroit techno, will tell you that it's the only intelligent form of techno. Most people think that the harder, faster, less musical forms of techno, void of melodies, is pure techno. Other people would say it's "acid-trance" or "gabba-techno." But someone who listens to gabba might call it house.

JF: What about jungle and drum and bass?

BC: Jungle is an old form. The early stuff was just sped-up breaks with vocals, and as it developed, they replaced the sampled vocals with ragga rap and took the bass beat out of it.

There are maybe a few tracks where you can say, this is jungle, or this is drum and bass, but mostly you'll have a hard time finding two DJs who will agree on exactly where one ends and the other begins. The term jungle started to become unfashionable and so people started to call it drum and bass. I find that most of the new drum and bass has begun to use really beautiful harmonies and melodies, and sometimes they'll have live MCs rapping over it.

JF: What's current, what are people listening to now?

BC: It depends on where you live. In Toronto, you'll hear a lot of jungle and drum and bass in the clubs. On the West Coast, you hear mostly progressive/trance and breaks. In San Francisco, they're playing a lot of deep house, which is a sparser form of house. In Los Angeles now, because of the influence of people like Moontribe, you will hear a lot of Hard trance that they are starting to call Desert trance or Mojave.

[Brent plays a track to illustrate the evolution of house. He calls it an early '80s crossover of acid house and disco. The rhythm is definitely disco, the vocals are heavily processed, and the instrumentation is made up of high-end synth sounds. He describes it as early house/early acid house, early techno/late disco.]

BC: I can play that at parties and people will ask me where I bought that new track, not realizing that it's 15 years old. A lot of DJs are discovering old tracks and playing them again. There is a long evolution of house music, a lot of turns and new directions as it tried to find its way. A lot of those experiments just died off.

JF: I've read that house is anything between 125 bpm [beats per minute, which indicates a song's tempo] to 140 bpm, and trance is anything faster than 140 bpm but not above 170 bpm. What about classifying by bpms?

BC: You might be able to get away with that, but there are lots of examples that don't follow that description. You can take a really clean breaks song, and if you slow it down enough it becomes hip-hop or trip-hop, and if you speed it up enough it becomes drum and bass or jungle. The speed does relate to it, but no more than the harmonies or any other elements of the music.

JF: How would you classify yourself as a DJ?

BC: Some people say I'm a trance DJ, some people say I'm a techno DJ or I'm a breaks DJ. It's whatever they hear in my music.

JF: *Do you preplan your sets?*

BC: No. A lot of people do, but I like to work in a more esoteric way. I like to figure out the energy in the room. When I've got a bad crowd, something about it feeds back to me and gives me less energy and makes me feel really drained. If that happens, I will try to shift the music to connect with the crowd. If I'm on a build that is not working, I might do three short songs that vary in style, gauge the reaction to give me some idea where the crowd it at, and begin the build again. If I work a whole night like that, struggling to connect with the crowd, I go home totally drained of energy. But normally I can figure it out and make it work. You can be a good technical DJ and program your nights. If you are playing at a party where everyone likes your music, you will do great, but if you always do that, you can become too egocentric, and the music it not allowed to grow the way it's supposed to grow.

The person who taught me was DJ Mindkind from Toronto, and he would never let me program my nights. He would never let me repeat a mix either and if I did, he would threaten to fire me. Every record should have more energy than the one before it. You can do that with speed or freshness and it doesn't necessarily have to be a nice long mix; sometimes a complete, dead drop out with a new sound coming up underneath will increase the energy. I try to follow the patterns that I've seen music take over the years. It comes in waves, with one thing trailing off and another new sound coming up at the same time.

DANCE MUSIC DEFINITIONS

The following descriptions merely outline basic electronic music styles. New variations are created every day.

House

House is the original electronic incarnation of disco. House typically runs around 120 bpm and uses a 4/4 time sequence with an 8-bar repeating cycle. A heavy kick drum anchors the beat, which alternates in a 1/3 pattern with a high hat accent. Like its disco roots, house features vocal choruses, real instrumentation, and has more of a traditional song structure.

Acid House

Acid house is an evolution of house characterized by high-pitched screaming "acid sounds" created by a Roland TB-303 bass line machine. These new psychedelic sounds were found to be particularly effective while under the influence of acid (LSD) and the hard, uncompromising samples produced a hypnotic effect.

Progressive House

Originating in England, progressive house was originally a blend of German trance and house. More electronic sounds are used in progressive house, like analog synths, which brings it closer to techno than the more soulful house. Generally faster than house, progressive house also features big dramatic builds, crescendos, and breakdowns.

Deep House

Also known as "deep disco," deep house is one of the earliest incarnations of house. When you strip away the vocals and organ sounds of traditional house music, you are left with the deep soulful extended grooves of deep house, driven by a deep throbbing bass line firmly rooted in the black American soul tradition.

Diva House

Diva house is a form of house developed in gay clubs. Diva house is dramatic, campy house built around operatic vocal samples.

Techno

An electronic evolution of house developed in Detroit, techno uses the 4/4 beat structure of house to build predominantly percussive tracks that use purely electronic sounds. Techno was originally influenced by the European electro sounds of Kraftwerk and electronic tracks from the Italo label in Italy.

Dub

In 1973, King Tubby, musician, studio owner, and engineer, turned the Kingston, Jamaica, music scene upside down. Reggae had always provided instrumental cuts, but his use of EQ, delay, sound effects, and a single-minded inventiveness elevated the instrumental as a creative art form. His instrument was the mixing console. His dub cuts of popular records of the time were in great demand. Many took his cue and experimented, with various degrees of success. By today's standards, the equipment used was more than primitive, but the music of this period sparks like no other. Today many of these techniques are added to other forms of electronic dance music.

Gabba Techno

Gabba techno originated in Holland; *gabba* means *buddy* or *mate* in Dutch. Gabba is four-beat hardcore that's hard as hell and fast, fast, fast, featuring distorted 240 bpm kick drums and big bass drum sounds. It's still popular in Holland and Belgium.

Trance

Trance is an evolution from progressive house and techno. Trance is designed to take the listener on an inner journey and features extended journey motifs with repeating and cyclic hypnotic elements. Trance also tends to be more densely layered and intense than techno.

Goa/Psy Trance

Goa trance takes its name from Goa, India; this is an incarnation of trance, with a more complex texture of psychedelic sounds woven into a kaleidoscopic tapestry. Goa tracks tend to be finished, complete pieces of music and are therefore less conducive to beat mixing. The beat is a steady 4/4 kick but is often buried in layers of analog sounds.

Hardcore

Hardcore is devolution of techno from the U.K. The original form used high speed, 3/4 time, and sampled break beats as its rhythmic base; it was also known as U.K. break beat. In 1992-93, another form called Four-Beat used a 4/4 rhythm. Also characterized by a Roland TR-909 kick drum through a distortion pedal, hardcore is dense, fast, and aggressive; it's mostly listened to in England, Belgium, and some Eastern Bloc countries.

Old School/Old Skool

Old school or old skool is the original break beat form from England that led to hardcore. Old school features a 3/4, sampled break beat as the main rhythm track. Though old school is distinctly different rhythmically, it retains many of the other original elements of house. This form was popular in England in the late '80s and has since disappeared.

Jungle

Originated in London, England by black urban musicians, jungle merges a syncopated hip-hop rhythm with dub reggae bass lines and sampled break beats. As with hardcore, sped-up samples of other records are also incorporated for the rhythm tracks, giving jungle a dense and complicated rhythmic base.

Drum and Bass

Drum and bass is a direct progression from jungle, although it is hard to say where one ends and the other begins. Mostly drum and bass is used for later recordings, while jungle describes older recordings. Generally speaking, drum and bass tends to be less complex rhythmically than jungle, with more of an emphasis on the drum and bass tracks.

Ambient

A term coined by Brian Eno, ambient is essentially electronic atmosphere music designed to relax the listener with its soothing vibes. Generally under 90 bpm or totally beatless, Ambient music takes you on a relaxing or thoughtful journey using a variety of sounds, from wind and whale sound samples to richly textured electronic landscapes.

Trip-Hop

Trip-hop is very slowed-down, instrumental hip-hop. The syncopated hip-hop beat is slowed down to 100 bpm or less and layered with the electronic, spacey sounds usually associated with ambient music. Made popular by musicians like Tricky and Massive Attack, trip-hop has been described as hip-hop in a flotation tank.

Break Beat

Originally invented by DJ Kool Herc by isolating percussive breaks from soul records, which formed the basis of hip-hop and rap. In recent years, however, electronic musicians have reinvented the concept by isolating "breaks" from house and techno tracks, creating something quite different. The syncopated hip-hop rhythm has been dropped and the galloping Break beat is hung on the 4/4 beat used by house and techno.

Garage

Named after the Paradise Garage club in New York, and New York's answer to Chicago house. Predominantly vocal-oriented house music, garage was the blending of house records with a wide variety of other sources including techno tracks, soul records and even rock and roll songs, resulting in a unique form also known as the Jersey Sound (because New Jersey is where many of the artists and producers came from).

Bhangra

Bhangra meshes traditional Punjabi folk songs and drumming with electronic house rhythms.

Chutney Soca

Chutney Soca comes from Trinidad and mixes Indian style melodies with a fast electronic Calypso beat.

Electro

Popular in the early '80s in New York, electro is an early form of hip-hop that marries syncopated rhythms with more techno-type sounds. Electro runs around 120 bpm and features the kick and the snare sounds from a Roland 808.

Tribal

Tribal is a type of house that incorporates sounds from Third World cultures. A heavy tribal beat is layered with sounds and flavors from the world's indigenous people.

[1] (Source: Brian Chin, Rhino Records)

[2] (Source: Used by permission, Jasonic/Meta Vibes)

[3] (Source: Brent Cunningham, University at Buffalo Reporter)

[4] (Source: Rob Swift of The X-ecutioners, *WIRE* Magazine)

[5] (Source: John Bush, All-Music Guide)

[6] (Source: Used by permission, Jasonic/Meta Vibes)

[7] (Source: Used by permission, Jasonic/Meta Vibes)

[8] (Source: John Bush, All-Music Guide)

[9] (Source: Used by permission, 5am-Hyperactive Media)

[10] (Source: Used by permission, Jasonic/Meta Vibes)

[11] (Source: Used by permission, Jasonic/Meta Vibes)

The Remix Phenomenon

THE BASICS

Remixing is the art of creating an alternate version of a song or instrumental piece of music. Early methods such as manual tape splicing and live mixing have given way to a dazzling array of digitally-based tools, such as hard disk recorders and digital audio editing computer programs, that can make remixing a much easier and more powerful process. The hard disk recorder, be it a hardware box or a computer program, digitizes the music into waveforms; then displays these graphically. (Fig. #10) These waveforms can be edited in many ways, including "cut and paste" techniques that are similar to how words are rearranged in a word processor. The music actually becomes digital information, and therefore can be manipulated in a virtually endless variety of ways.

Fig. #10: Graphic representation of an audio waveform. The vertical axis represents amplitude (level), while the horizontal axis represents time.

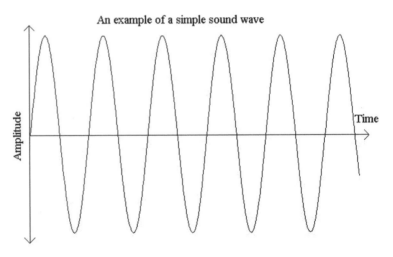

An example of a simple sound wave

Another key component of modern remixing is the use of electronic digital instruments such as keyboards, drum machines, samplers, and effects processors. By using a universal electronic language protocol known as MIDI (Musical Instrument Digital Interface), electronic instruments can communicate with one another as well as with computers and hard disk recorders. MIDI data can also be recorded, and play back through MIDI-

Remix: The Electronic Music Explosion

compatible instruments; the process is similar to how a player piano "reads" data from a paper roll, then uses this to trigger the keys needed to play a piece. With MIDI, however, the paper roll is replaced by computer memory, and sounds are triggered electronically, not by physically pressing the keys.

As many remixers began their careers as DJs, the knowledge of dance music is essential in the creation of a good production. They are also familiar with technology and mixing, and generally are very comfortable with today's amazing music machines.

Fig. #11: MIDI gear diagram

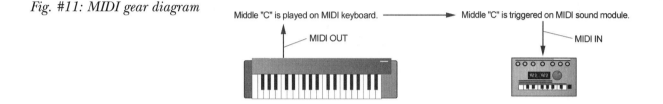

Middle "C" is played on MIDI keyboard. ⟶ Middle "C" is triggered on MIDI sound module.

MIDI OUT   MIDI IN

Music industry manufacturers recognize the impact of DJs, remixers and the dance culture in general; and carefully tailor their products to appeal to this new, emerging market. Kids learning to spin records in the bedroom long to be DJs, and DJs generally long to become remixers. Like a rite of passage in dance culture, becoming known as a remixer signals a metamorphosis from DJ to Remix artist.

Ironically, development of the "dance culture sound" likely has something to do with economics. Musicians were the primary targets for the early electronic gizmos that were first introduced to the marketplace. Always quick to adopt cutting edge technology, musicians were more inclined to accept radically new products than other types of consumers. Music technology began to change very quickly as newer, better models became available. For example, as the '80s progressed, analog gear that is now considered classic such as the Roland TB-303 Bass Line, Minimoog synthesizer, Linn 9000 drum machine, etc. were eventually cast aside after the novelty wore off and often were thought of as poor imitations of real-sounding instruments. As digital technology was introduced, the new goal of many manufacturers was to create products that made the most realistic sounds as possible to meet the demand of musicians.

Analog instruments (such as the ARP Odyssey and the Sequential Circuits Prophet-5) that originally found favor with rock musicians of the '70s eventually gave way to the newer and more sophisticated digital instruments. When the Yamaha DX7 was introduced in 1983, older analog synths were suddenly out of style.

Older models were relegated to the second-hand bins, pawnshops, and garage sales. The less affluent could obtain this gear at reasonable prices and began to tinker with the sounds. Using these instruments as the building blocks for recording and MIDI sequencing (the process of recording and playing back MIDI data), production became more accessible. With a good musical sense and a relatively low investment, music production began to move from the large established studios to the bedroom or the basement.

Around this time, older equipment began to surface in other styles of music. For example, hip-hop built much of its sound around the Roland TR-606 and TR-808 drum machines. (Legend has it that the TR-808 became popular with hip-hop artists because a music store in New York had received a large shipment of these drum machines from Roland, and left the boxes outside temporarily while they made space in the store. Before they could be moved inside, there was a downpour, which ruined the packaging. Unable to return the units to Roland, the store put them on sale at a ridiculously low price, and all the drum machines sold out instantly to emerging musicians looking for bargains).

Often older synths were used to create fat analog bass lines. Gradually these instruments became associated with the genre. German pioneers Kraftwerk began experimenting with the new electronic equipment in the early '70s, and ultimately played a huge role in the evolution of modern dance sound. Also, the development of techno music drew on the machine-like qualities and outdated sounds of the older (and at that time, inexpensive) early electronic instruments.

The trend toward less expensive home production ultimately spawned a Remix revolution. Many of today's hit recordings are produced in home studios. With the advent of more affordable computers, software, and MIDI gear, remixing is often better suited to the home environment.

Let's take a closer look at what actually happens in a Remix. The following section "What is a Remix?" was written by James Lumb, a musician, remixer and founder of the legendary electronica band *Electric SkyChurch* in Los Angeles. He has been intimately involved in electronic music production since the mid-'80s. Producing from his home studio based in Hollywood, California, he was instrumental in the formation of the "Moontribe" Events. It's generally thought that James was responsible for coining the term "Electronica." For more information on James and his band, surf to **http://www.skychurch.com**.

WHAT IS A REMIX?

Article by James Lumb

If DJs are the rock stars of the 21st Century, then Remix is the folk music of the information age. Remixing is the electro-garage-cover band of tomorrow. Remixing is a musical participation sport; anybody can do it.

Remix has become a broad slang term in the music industry that could refer to anything from obscure experimental electronica to Cher's latest "hit." Old tracks get recycled into new tracks – a new art form emerges – sonic collage.

On its most basic level, all you need to do is "DJ" music for yourself and your friends. That huge collection of records, tapes and CDs you've invested in over the years is "software." You (presumably) own that musical software, and are entitled to use it. Hook up all those old stereo components to that Radio Shack mixer and start crossfading between tracks. Tape what comes out and you have a Remix. Add a computer, chop it up, trick it out with effects, and you still have a Remix. Remixing is a way of exploring your own musical history, and presenting it to someone else.

In the acoustic folk music tradition, artists trade licks and melodies. In the emerging electronic folk music tradition, artists sample each other. It's a mixed bag of legal mumbo-jumbo, but no one can stop you from non-commercial DJing with your own private record collection.

Of course, there are more advanced methods of mixing and remixing. Electronic musical tools that blur the lines between the "musician" and "DJ" are finding their way to the market-place.

Remixing co-evolved with DJ culture. Although DJing has been around since radio stations first went on the air, it really blossomed into an art form during the late '60s, as discotheques became popular. With the introduction of inexpensive drum machines and samplers in the '80s, DJing exploded. All of a sudden it became possible to create music with a machine-steady tempo that was easy to "beat match" (i.e., segue from one recording to another while maintaining a constant tempo). The art of DJing naturally co-evolved alongside machine-based music for a simple reason – live performance of electronic music was an expensive pain in the ass. Producers became DJs out of necessity as a way to present their studio tracks to an audience.

Now that's all changing. Electronic music is getting ever less expensive to create. Equipment manufacturers are building hybrid musical instruments that blur the lines between remixing and live performance. DJs are not limited to turntables and mixers. Turntables are the sound sources that feed compressors, performance effects, phrase samplers and a host of emerging techno goodies that make live "DJ performances" unique. More and more, live instruments find their way into the mix. Remember, synths and samplers are driven by musical software. CDs and records are also valid pieces of musical software.

Not to be confused with radio DJs, Remix DJs normally use two turntables, CD, or Minidisc players and a small mixer to "cross-fade" seamlessly between recordings. They can speed up or slow down a record's tempo so that the "beats" within the music on one turntable match up with the beats (rhythm) from a very different record on another turntable. In dance music, this allows the presentation of endlessly flowing music. The beats never stop (and neither do the dancers). DJ-oriented dance tracks rarely contain tempo changes, which makes beat matching easier. Timing changes within the music are executed "live" by the DJ during the "performance" or "mix."

Over the years, putting a DJ set together out of other people's music has become recognized as a narrative art form. A good DJ set is often referred to as a "journey" because it takes the listener to another place. Think of it as a "sound only" movie made of records. Electronic artists depend on DJs to bring their music to the masses.

So what does this have to do with Remix? Technically, a Remix is not an original song. A Remix is an alternate version of an original piece that usually, but not always, is created as a "musical" tool for DJs. Remixes differ from covers by incorporating sampled bits of audio from the original song. A Remix can be sampled from any piece of music – electronic music, jazz, rock, funk, classical or world music – anything is fair game.

If you already produce electronic music, but want to start remixing your songs for DJs, remember that DJs are looking for tracks that work on the dance floor, and can be mixed, remixed, twisted and morphed. Often a simple track that may sound "unfinished" to you sounds great when mixed with other tracks by a good DJ. Remixes are often so far removed from the original that they become new pieces of music. Opportunity for creative expression is definitely "in the mix."

Perhaps you already own some keyboards and a drum machine, or a full studio. If so, you can start right away. Some of the most successful Remixes in the world were created on a sampler with built-in sequencing and effects.

If you own a studio and like working with other people, you might consider adding a DJ rig as an instrument, much like a guitar rig or drum set. A simple DJ rig will cost anywhere between US$400 and $1,500. Invite a bunch of DJs over and your studio will be churning out DJ tracks in no time. DJs like to hang out where the gear is – getting the DJs to go home will be your main problem.

Typical commercial Remix sessions might go something like this. You start with either a source DAT that contains bits of music, or just sample the original song from vinyl or CD. Pick a few bits you like, and discard the rest. Those bits are your "samples."

Once your audio samples have been loaded into computer or keyboard sampler, they can be chopped up, rearranged, and looped into "grooves." This way, you can change the pitch, tempo, and dynamics of the original samples to fit your ideas.

There are no rules, but often a producer might start building up the groove one layer at a time by adding drums, then bass, synthesizer, and sound effects. Once you have grooves you like, use a sequencer (this can be a computer sequencer or a dedicated keyboard sequencer) to arrange your grooves into a song.

How do you keep your tracks from sounding like every other song out there? Drum grooves can be obnoxiously "common," so adding some good filtering and effects will help with the piece's texture. Performance effects (such as the "Electrix" line of signal processors) can really liven up repetitive beats. Hook them up between your turntables, CD players, or DAT machine and resample the music while twiddling the performance knobs on the effects boxes. Using filters on drumbeats, or morphing beats through a "vocoder" (a device that allows instruments to "talk" by impressing vocal characteristics onto instrumental sounds) can produce amazingly original results from sampled material. With performance effects, you can quickly create a new groove out of an old song without having to spend hours chopping up beats.

On the other hand, creating a solid groove from scratch takes time and patience. For example, if you have a great 136 BPM loop but you want to incorporate it into a song that moves along at 130 BPM, the process of time-correcting and beat-shifting can be very difficult. In the past, producers tempo-corrected samples manually, cutting, pasting, pitch shifting, and stretching until they obtained the right results. This often involved hours spent hunched over a computer keyboard. Fortunately, new computer software optimized for making grooves is now available, and can greatly streamline the process. Steinberg's "Recycle" (for Mac or PC) will automatically chop your samples into small bits (individual notes), then load them back into your sampler for playback via MIDI. Once your sample has been chopped up you can change the timing of individual notes or beats – this makes it really easy to hit a steady groove. For instance, you can take a sample of a live drummer and change the groove from straight up to shuffled and back again. This program has revolutionized drum sequencing, and the drum and bass dance genre is a testament to its power.

Other sample editing programs such as Bias' "Peak," Steinberg's "Wavelab," and Sonic Foundry's "Sound Forge" give you a set of tools for time-stretching, beat matching and morphing loops. Your beats become flexible in time and pitch, and can sound kind of rubbery with enough processing. Stretching out a sample over time without changing its pitch has a "sound" all its own. There's even a program, Sonic Foundry's "Acid," that's designed solely for creating groove-based music. You can load audio samples of just about any tempo or key into the program, which will automatically convert them to the desired tempo or key "on the fly." The result is nothing short of magical, and eliminates the need to do any manual manipulation whatsoever.

In addition to software-based sample editors, there are also software-based groove synthesizers. Steinberg's "Rebirth" may look like a video game, but it sounds like an expensive vintage "acid house" rig. It contains two virtual TB-303 Bass Line synths alongside two virtual drum machines (TR-808 and TR-909). If you want to learn about drum machines without the high cost of hardware, it's a good place to start—and you can make some great grooves.

Want to play the track you mixed on your computer this morning tonight at a party? Lack the time and patience to have expensive vinyl test pressings made? OK. Just add a CD burner to your computer, mix it, burn it, give it to the DJ, and your homemade CD becomes the freshest track at the party.

If CDs are not "interactive" enough for you, and you plan to play out live, you might want to leave your computer at home. For now, computers tend to crash on stage under poor conditions (e.g., when some dork plugs the lights into your power strip). Laptops with a good power conditioner can be a better option. Also, taking your 1500-pound studio out every night can be a drag. (I know this from personal experience!) Fortunately, there is an emerging "easier way." Every major synth manufacturer has a "groove" box of some sort on the market. They usually incorporate sampling, looping, time-stretching, drum and synth sequencing into one box with some performance controls. You can knock out a Remix at home and play it out live the same day. Mixing and tweaking "live" at the machine level sounds great. You can tailor the individual sounds to fit the room and crowd. Groove boxes allow you to get a lot closer to your audience than you can with records by themselves. Groove boxes, keyboards, records, and live acoustic instruments can combine to make some really amazing performances.

A one-person live Remix rig might contain a set of DJ turntables, CD players, and a sampling mixer. Add a microphone, a groove box, and a couple of signal processors, and the level of originality soars higher.

The future is now. Remix is not limited to dance music; whatever you like is fair game. It doesn't matter if you're into Bob Marley or Beethoven, if it can be sampled, looped, twisted, and spit back out as something new, go for it!

If you fear that Remix will destroy music as we know it, think again. Remix is saving music. As DJs and producers sample bits and pieces of the past into their new tracks, they are acting as archivists who present our recorded musical history to a new audience. It's common for electronic music fans to seek out the source of a sample and buy the original. As the Remix genre becomes more sophisticated, musical bibliographies have begun springing up in liner notes of new releases. Miles Davis records are sold to kids who discovered his music through a sample on the dance floor. If anything, remixing is causing a musical renaissance.

So take that record you so carefully recorded and release it, but Remix it as well. Then show up at a party with some decks and play it for your friends. Let your friends get up on the decks and play their favorite records for you. Good tracks are hard to find, and everyone has a favorite song no one else knows about. Share! Dance! Play! Remix is a party participation sport!

Traditional DJ Tools

Traditional DJ tools that have developed through the years continue to keep their basic layout of two or three channels with a crossfader. Specialized DJ mixers by manufacturers like Numark (known especially for their highly respected and influential DM1775A and DM1975 digital sampler mixers), Gemini, Rane, and Vestax have long been the staple for DJs. Other musical instrument manufacturers, perhaps more associated with strictly professional equipment, have recognized the potential of the DJ market and have recently introduced DJ mixers. Soundcraft, Peavey, Pioneer, and Roland have all invested heavily into this exploding market.

DJs initially viewed CD players with suspicion and a lot of skepticism surrounded the first dual CD from Numark, introduced in 1990 and featuring pitch control. The DJs preference for vinyl meant that this particular format required some time to really take off. When it finally happened, it didn't take long for many other manufacturers to introduce similar products. Denon raised the standard of DJ-friendly CD players, then Vestax, Gemini and Numark soon followed their lead. Most recently the Japanese giant Pioneer took the CD player market by storm with their CDJ500, a truly radical piece of equipment that was quickly accepted by the market.

Roland has spent millions in recent years to develop their *Groove* line of products. The new Electrix line, Akai samplers, Emu sound modules, Zoom drum machines and a myriad computer sequencers, hard disk recorders and editing software are enjoying huge popularity in home recording studios, from where most electronic music still emanates.

GETTING STARTED IN THE BUSINESS

Article by Troy Wolfe

Troy Wolfe, is a writer and DJ living in Victoria, B.C. Recently, he was one of the first North American DJs to play in Seoul, South Korea.

The electronic/dance music phenomenon is certainly one of the fastest-growing markets in the North American music industry. Already well-established in Europe, it is responsible there for the conception of countless bedroom studios and an explosive proliferation of DJs to the point that you can't swing a record bag as you walk down the street without hitting at least a few. The fame of DJs in Europe is pretty much on a par with that of pop stars in North America. The result of this rapid growth and interest in making and playing electronic music is that there are more choices than ever when it comes to choosing the gear that you may want to use. The purpose of this section is to help you choose the right gear in the right price range for the kind of work you want to do.

The first decision is whether you want to play vinyl records or CDs as a DJ. Whether you would like to mix them together in clubs or at parties, or whether you want to be involved in actually creating the music yourself. This could be taking it from initial creative impulses to actually performing your tracks live or seeing them preserved in vinyl or CD. A lot of music producers, especially in dance music, will begin their careers as DJs, buying music produced by others and learning first-hand what works on a dance floor and what clears people off the floor to get a drink or go to the bathroom. Others will want to be a part of the complete creative process, making their own music from scratch and thereby getting their ideas out into the world for others to play. Either path will involve spending some money on the gear you will use to express yourself musically.

The Entry Level DJ

When it comes to DJ gear your choices are pretty simple. The three basic requirements are two turntables (or CD players), and a mixer with at least two channels. You also need a sound system to hear what you are playing, as well as a pair of headphones; you may already have these if you have a decent home stereo.

There is a good range of inexpensive turntables, look for ones with direct drive and pitch control. Options include the Numark TT-1910, Gemini XL- 500 or PT-1000, and American DJ TTD-2500. These units all retail for under US$200. To mix CDs, you need two CD players with variable pitch. Typical models include the American DJ DCD-200, Gemini CD-9500, and Next! CD-5000, all retailing for around US$700 a pair. Numark also offers their CDM 34 (Fig. 12) for about US$1,100 which contains two CD players and a mixer in one compact unit.

Fig. #12: The Numark CDM34 is a relatively high-end CD-oriented DJ machine.

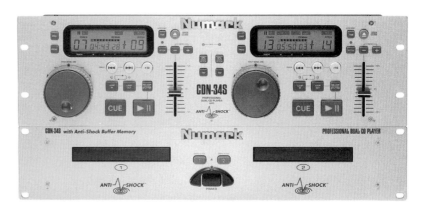

The other essential piece of DJ gear is the mixer that allows you to crossfade one track seamlessly into another, creating a sensation on the dance floor (of course) in the process. The bare minimum requirement is two phono channels and a level control for each one, although even inexpensive mixers will commonly have three channels. Most also offer two- or three-band equalizers (tone controls) on each channel, allowing more complete control over the sound. Different mixers will have different "feels" in how the controls work, and have subtly different sound qualities. Some of the less expensive mixers are the Gemini BPM 250, Vestax PMC-03A and PMC-005A MK2, the Next! PDJ-22, CMX-460 and the Numark DM-2000, all available for under US$400.

Fig. #13: Gemini
BPM 250 DJ Mixer

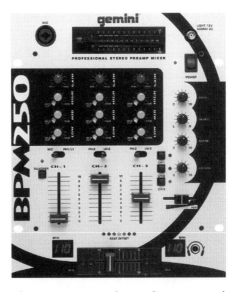

The Entry Level Producer/Remixer

If you are a novice who has little or no musical experience and no equipment, your main concerns are most likely choosing gear that:

• Is relatively easy to learn how to use
• Is versatile and can performs lots of different functions
• Involves minimal financial investment

Anyone who has ever spent time looking through the manuals included with some of the more sophisticated synths, samplers, or effects processors quickly gets the idea that you would have an easier time reading the complete works of Shakespeare in Danish. If you aren't familiar with the jargon common to electronic instruments, then you may have a difficult time completing even the simplest operations. Some manufacturers, though, provide a very user-friendly interface that is intended to make life easy for the beginner. The Roland Grooveboxes and the new Electrix products come to mind as machines that allow the user to operate them almost intuitively and get satisfying results. Both provide a wide array of sounds, accessible through user-friendly hardware controls that can create or modify tracks pretty quickly.

The next element to consider is versatility. This can be approached in two different ways. A computer with decent processor speed and memory is one of the most versatile and powerful tools available to an aspiring producer. A wide assortment of software can take the place of hardware samplers, synthesizers, mixing boards, sequencers and effects processors. For example, Cakewalk Pro Audio (around US$400, Windows only) incorporates a MIDI sequencer, virtual mixing console, hard disk recording, and 32-bit effects processing ability. Cubase VST and Logic Audio (Mac or Windows) are also powerful tools that can turn your computer into a digital music workstation. It may be necessary, however, to upgrade your computer's existing sound capabilities and memory to make the most of any music software you install. If you don't own a computer, however, then buying one might be prohibitively expensive, especially when you factor in the cost of software and accessories.

The other option is to buy some select pieces of gear that give you a lot of bang for your buck. One of the most versatile stand-alone machines is the sampler. Armed with a good sound library and/or a desire to invent your own sounds, a sampler can replace many of the functions of a synth, drum machine, sequencer, and effects unit. Not all samplers will be able to perform all of these duties but most will tackle at least two of them. Two great all-round samplers, the Yamaha A-3000 and Akai MPC-2000, both retail for around US$2,000. For a no-frills machine, check out the Akai U-40 "Riff-O-Matic" or the Boss SP-202, both cost less than US$500. For something more feature-laden, check out the Roland SP-808. It costs around US$2000 but includes an analog synth simulator, an 8-track hard-disk recorder, built in ZIP drive for storage to ZIP disks, and effects.

Some affordable synths, such as the Yamaha CS1X or Korg N5, also perform a variety of duties. They can offer synthesizer sounds along with drum kits, but also typically include built-in sequencers and effects. If they're not rack-mount units, then they also provide a keyboard that can trigger other MIDI-compatible units as well. If you are using more than one piece of gear, or even if you are using a single piece with lots of outputs, you will need some kind of mixing board to provide control. You will want to adjust the level, pan (stereo placement), and EQ (tonality) of each sound you use on your track.

If you don't have a computer and therefore can't take advantage of virtual mixing, you may want to invest in a small mixing board. The US$500 Mackie MS1202-VLZ is a 12-channel board with a 3-band EQ and stereo bus on each channel; it should suffice for anyone with a simple personal studio. One final consideration is what you will use to record your tracks. The simplest and cheapest solution is to make cassette copies, but cassette tapes are pretty noisy and lose a little bit of their fidelity every time you play them. A digital recording device is much better. If you own a computer, there's excellent software for digitally recording audio right onto your hard drive. If you also have a recordable CD drive, you can then "burn" that audio onto a CD. A good alternative is a DAT player/recorder, standalone CD recorder, or Minidisc. While Minidisc's fidelity is not quite up to that of CDs, they're small and portable, which makes them ideal for recording your own "real-world" samples.

If you're getting started in DJing or personal music production, the important thing is to lay out your goals and find equipment that you can afford and will help you fulfill those goals. Don't be afraid to ask for advice from other DJs, musicians, and equipment dealers, or post questions on Internet forums. Other people have been in your situation themselves and can offer you invaluable information.

The Intermediate DJ

If you can invest more money into your DJ rig, the extra bucks will likely buy you gear with better quality construction and better sound. For turntables, there has been (until recently) only one choice for the serious DJ: the Technics SL-1200 and, to a lesser extent, the SL-1500. Both are extremely rugged, high quality decks and are found in the vast majority of clubs, bedrooms, and party venues. However, the new Numark TT-1 turntable is challenging the 1200's dominance thanks to an equal level of quality and some new features, such as increased pitch control range via a joystick controller. Either option will cost US$750 – $850 per turntable. For those interested in mixing CDs, professional-quality dual CD players, such as the Denon 2000F-MK-3 or 2500F, will cost between US$1,000–$2,000. The 2500F even offers some limited sampling capabilities.

Two top-of-the-line mixers are the Pioneer DJM-500 and the Roland DJ-2000. Both have four channels, with three of these being phono inputs, allowing the DJ to apply real-time effects (e.g., delay, flanger, filter, etc.) along with whatever is being played.

If you thought that electronic musical instruments were a recent development, think again. As early as 1913, the Italian composer Luigi Russolo featured the industrial noises and rhythms of factories and machinery in a piece called "Art of Noises." This may well have been the first industrial music, but it was in the '20s that the first electronic instruments, the Theremin and the Ondes Martenot, were invented. Composers such as Honegger, Messiaen, Milhaud, Dutilleux and Varèse all composed for the Ondes Martenot. The Theremin was also widely used, and probably best known for the ethereal and eerie high-pitched wailing sounds used in numerous horror and science fiction movies in the '50s. Oskar Sala was another early electronic pioneer who in 1928, together with Dr. Friedrich Trautwein, built an electronic musical instrument called the Trautonium; a monophonic device based on an oscillator with a glimmer lamp. The Trautonium could continuously alter tone color via a horizontally stretched wire that was pressed against a metal rod beneath it.

In 1950, Sala invented a more sophisticated electronic instrument called the Mixturtrautonium, which he used to compose the music for Alfred Hitchcock's thriller "The Birds." In 1926 Jorg Mager built an electronic instrument called the Spharophon, and later created the Partiturophon and the Kaleidophon. And in the '40s came the Solovox and the Clavioline, the Electronic Sakbutt, the Melochord, the Multimonica, the Polychord organ, the Tuttivox and the Marshall organ.

As new musical tools were invented, the musicians of the day were inspired to think about music in a different way. The sounds being produced by the new technology were unlike anything that had gone before and gave musicians a new musical palette. A good example of an early experiment, John Cage's "Imaginary Landscape #1" composed in 1939, was the first piece of music to be reproduced electronically.

With the introduction of the Moog synthesizer in 1964, the golden age of electronic music was born. The rock musicians of the '60s were already experimenting wildly with both instrumentation and form, so they had no hesitation in embracing these new tools. Shortly afterwards, the Mellotron was invented which was the first keyboard that actually played samples. However, the first real digital sampler was The Fairlight CMI (Computer Musical Instrument), invented in 1979 by two Australians, Kim

Ryrie and Peter Vogul. This crude and bulky instrument was first used by the likes of Mike Oldfield, Stevie Wonder, The Pet Shop Boys and the legendary Jean Michel Jarre.

Excerpt from "Rave Culture", by Jimmy Fritz.- Used by permission

Although hundreds of manufactures have built instruments used in various forms of electronic dance production, there seems to be an "A-list" of the most used and preferred. Time and time again, you begin to notice certain sounds associated with certain styles of music. The more you listen, the more you can begin to pick out these sounds and learn to know which electronic instrument was used. Let's look at some of the most popular instruments that make up the world of dance sounds.

Drum Machines

Dance music's beat is its most important characteristic, and much modern dance music is based on drum machines. Often using sampled drum sounds, these devices are actually small sequencers optimized for creating drum patterns. These drum patterns can be linked with others to create a song with different sections. While techno music is often criticized for having monotonous drum parts, dancers appreciate the hypnotic effects of the beat that becomes a constant underpinning for the entire dance experience. The following is a brief history and summary of the devices most closely associated with dance production; for more information, surf to The Drum Machine Museum at http://www.drummachine.com.

The Rhythmicon (or Polyrhythmophone; 1930)

In 1916, while American avant-garde composer Henry Cowell was working with ideas of controlling cross rhythms and tonal sequences with a keyboard, he wrote several quartet type pieces that used combinations of rhythms and overtones that were not possible to play without some kind of mechanical control. (Or as he said, "un-performable by any known human agency and I thought of them as purely fanciful"). In 1930 Cowell introduced his idea to Leon Theremin, the inventor of the Theremin, and commissioned him to build him a machine capable of transforming harmonic data into rhythmic data and vice versa.

The Chamberlin Rhythmate

The Chamberlin Rhythmate was prototyped in 1948, and
produced in its first incarnation throughout the '50s. The first
model used loops of 1/4" tape that were pulled around with a
motor, and the "sounds" were played back with a series of tape
heads. It was the forerunner to the Mellotron.

The Linn Drum

Developed in 1979 by Roger Linn, the Linn LM1 was the world's
first commercially available programmable drum machine using
sampled sounds. (In the mid-'70s Paia Electronics produced a
true programmable drum machine using analog sounds; it was a
major influence on musician Peter Gabriel. In 1970, Craig
Anderton built a programmable electronic drum machine with
analog sounds, but all programming was done mechanically,
through switches). This debut product of Linn Electronics
started a revolution in popular music during the '80s. Originally
sold for $5,000 each, only about 500 were made, but those 500
owners were a "who's who" of the music industry. The 18 fixed
drum sounds were mostly recorded by local L.A. session
drummer Art Wood, and sampled at only 28 kHz using an 8 bit
non-linear format. Cymbals weren't included due to the high

cost of memory required to hold long sounds. The operating system allowed both real-time loop recording of rhythm patterns as well as step entry, and introduced innovations such as quantize, swing and creating songs by chaining patterns together.

Used by permission- The Drum Machine Museum

Roland-

Roland is probably the most widely accepted and in many ways the key manufacturer in the evolution of the modern dance sound. Founded in Japan by Ikutaro Kakehashi in 1972, Roland developed a series of drum machines and synthesizers ultimately creating the highly coveted classics that are still in use today. The following is a brief description of the models most associated with dance production.

TR-808

The Roland TR-808 (Fig. #15) was a revolutionary computer-controlled rhythm machine that offered up to 768 measures. In addition, this unit provided more percussive variations and more effects than virtually any other unit on the market at the time. If you had to label one piece of gear as the foundation of hip-hop production, the TR-808 would be it.

Fig. #15: The Roland TR-808 enjoyed only moderate success when it was introduced, but has become a much-coveted classic over the years.

It has been used by 808 State (whose name even references this legendary piece of gear), and by Aurora, Afrika Bambaataa, Aphex Twin, Beastie Boys, Bomb The Bass, Chris Carter, Phil Collins, D.A.V.E., DDR, D-Nice, Doctor Walker, Dr.Dre, The Drummer, Electronic Dream Planet, Warren G, Marvin Gaye, Paul Hardcastle, Whitney Houston, Jean Michel Jarre, Tom

Jones, KLF, KMFDM, Chris Liberator, Lisa Lisa & Cult Jam, Guy McAffer, N.W.A., Orbital, Panic On The Titanic, Plastik Man, Rei$$dorf Force, Rowland The Bastard, Insom Shalom, Sir Mix-A-Lot, Skinny Puppy, Snoop Doggy Dogg, and Mark Tyler.

TR-909

Much has been written and said about the impact of this machine when the house and techno scene emerged. Originally released in the mid-'80s, the TR-909 (Fig. #16) never had much initial success as the public craved real-sounding drums, so it was discontinued shortly after its introduction. Today it is serves as the foundation of house music production and is one of the most sought-after production machines on the market.

Fig. #16: The TR-909 is a staple of house and techno music.

TR-707

The Rhythm Composer TR-707 made the transition from analog to sampled sounds, and allowed programming four "Rhythm Tracks" or tunes (altogether 998 bars) from up to 64 user-created rhythm patterns. Each of the 15 digital drum voices is extremely realistic and has a separate output jack to allow for individual mixing, echo, or equalization. It is favored by groups like Aphex Twin, Big Black, Chemical Brothers Chris & Cosey - ex-Throbbing Gristle members on the album 'Techno Primitiv' Electronic Dream Planet, D.A.V.E., DDR, The Drummer, Tom Jenkinson of Squarepusher and Chaos Ad, KMFDM, Chris Liberator, Guy McAffer, Rowland The Bastard, and Mark Tyler.

R-70

Incorporating digital samples of classic analog drum sounds from the TR-808, 909 and the 707, the R70 provides an easy-to-use and effective alternative to purchasing high priced vintage instruments.

We'll let Roger Linn, from an interview on the Drum Machine Museum site, have the last word on drum machines: "People tend to buy drum machines for different reasons today. Most people today who wish to create a complex drum part will use a sequencer and sampler, whereas drum machines are purchased more by those who wish to play along with a steady drumbeat. I think that trend will continue.

"Regarding software products, Steinberg's Rebirth is the only software drum machine that seems to be selling well. There are still too many impediments with software products for most people: buggy and complex operating systems, computer sound card issues, and the [lack of] dedicated knobs or buttons. If the long term, many people will prefer a low-cost self-contained product that will work instantly when they turn it on, contains real knobs and controls, and that they don't have to share with a family member who happens to be typing a term paper."

Analog Synthesizers

And we'll also let Roger introduce the topic of vintage synthesizers: "It isn't vintage machines that are popular. It is analog synths that are popular. No one is buying vintage digital synths. People like analog synths because of a simple concept: you can easily mold the sound using a simple user interface. People don't like them because they're old; they like them because they're useful and they're going to keep buying them until they are no longer perceived to be useful."

The emergence of the modern synthesizer in the early '70s has run the gamut of musical styles; ranging from George Martin's use of the Moog in early Beatles tunes, to the overdone synth stacks of '70s' "progressive rock" bands. These keyboard synths and modules, along with drum machines, make up the heart of electronic music.

Analog synths offer warmer sounds compared to their digital counterparts, with the ability to easily modify sound parameters while the synth is being played. The older style "one knob per function" user interface costs much more to make than the 4 button/LCD interfaces found on so many modern synthesizers, but is vastly more effective and "friendly." The natural variability of analog circuitry is an added benefit to analog synths as long as you understand that the sound is constantly, and subtly, changing over time. The following list is but a brief overview of some of the classic analog synths that are favored by electronic musicians. Keep in mind uniqueness is the key; the weirder, the better.

THE CLASSICS: ANALOG SYNTHESIZERS

Sequential Circuts Prophet-5

Revolutionary for its time and now a classic, the Prophet-5 was one of the first affordable programmable, polyphonic analog synths on the market (prior to the Prophet-5, most synths were monophonic, or capable of producing only one voice at a time, and could not save their sounds in memory). The Prophet-5 contains five individual voices. For its principal sound sources each voice contains two VCO's (voltage controlled oscillators), OSC A and OSC B, and a white noise source which can be mixed into a resonant low-pass VCF (voltage controlled filter).

This instrument has been used by; Laurie Anderson, Rod Argent, Joan Armatrading, Wally Badarou, Dave Balfe of Teardrop Explodes, Dave Ball of Soft Cell, Tony Banks, Richard Barbieri, Katrina Bihan, Michael Boddicker, Andy Brown, Arthur Brown, Rabbit Bundrick, Damon Butcher, Kim Carnes, Bob Casale of Devo, Ian Catt, Clannad, Vince Clarke, Richard Coles of Communards, Phil Collins, Colourbox, Carl Cox, Crowded House, Steve Cunningham, Chris Franke of Tangerine Dream, Geoff Downes, George Duke, Electribe 101, Electronic, Anders Eljas of Abba, Vic Emerson, John Entwistle, Larry Fast, Johnny Fingers, Paul Fishman, Frontline Assembly, Peter Gabriel, and Philip Glass.

ARP 2600

With its oblong case and detachable lid, the ARP 2600 is a three-oscillator analog synthesizer complete with effects processing and amplification. Perhaps the most important ARP-implemented change came in 1975, when a modification from fellow synth designer Tom Oberheim (then only a designer of signal processors) was adopted on production models. The mod not only provided a form of duophony (one oscillator serving the low note and another the high), but also a delayed vibrato feature and a choice of single/multiple triggering. (Excerpted with permission from Keyfax: Omnibus Edition by Julian Colbeck, published by MixBooks).

This synthesizer was favored by 808 State, Tony Banks on "And Then There Were Three," The Beloved, Michael Boddicker, Arthur Brown, Richard Burgess, Chemical Brothers on "Dig Your Own Hole," Vince Clarke, Mike Cotten with the Tubes, Steve Cunningham, Jack Dangers of Meat Beat Manifesto, Depeche Mode, Electronic Dream Planet, John Entwistle (of The Who), Brian Gascoigne, Miquette Giraudy with Gong, and Roger Glover of Deep Purple.

Moog Modular

Bob Moog is a guiding pioneer in the development of electronic synthesizers. Initially expanding on the idea of the Theremin, Moog offered the first commercially available synthesizers in the early '60s. (Simultaneously on the West Coast, Don Buchla introduced the Buchla synthesizer, which relied on interfaces other than the standard keyboard and was favored more by avant-garde musicians such as Morton Subotnick than by pop musicians). Early models were awkward collections of modules, the size of refrigerators, with a blinding maze of patch cords and controls. Using the early Moog modules, the release of "Switched On Bach" by Wendy Carlos thrust the word "synthesizer" into the mainstream musical vocabulary.

Minimoog

Produced from 1970-1981, the idea of the Minimoog (Fig. #17) was to take some of the basic features of the modular instruments and integrate them into a compact performance synthesizer that could be programmed without patch cords. The Minimoog featured three voltage-controlled oscillators, a mixer, noise source, VCA, and a 24 dB/octave resonant filter whose "warm" sound is still coveted today. The Minimoog also had an external input that allowed external signals to be processed through the filter.

Fig. #17: The Minimoog, a true classic synthesizer (photo courtesy of William Blakeney).

As to who played this instrument, perhaps a more relevant question is who didn't! Minimoog enthusiasts included Thomas Dolby, Neil Doughty of REO Speedwagon (on "Ridin' The Storm Out"), Geoff Downes, George Duke (encased in plexiglass, lit internally, and capable of being worn like a guitar), Kris of Dweeb, Electronic Dream Planet, Keith Emerson, The Enid, Everything But the Girl, Tommy Eyre, Larry Fast, Baby Ford, Front Line Assembly, Lowell George, Dave Greenfield, Jan Hammer (the Minimoog, processed by distortion, was part of the secret of his famous guitar sound used on his albums and for scores for the TV shows such as "Miami Vice"), Herbie Hancock, Paul Hardcastle, Heatwave (on "Boogie Nights"), Steve Hillage (his was customized by Graham Wood), and Robert Hoffman on Michael Jackson's History.
Used by permission: www.synthmuseum.com

Korg MS-10

Used by Juan Atkins as the basis of his early productions, a style which ultimately became known as techno, the MS-10 (Fig, #18) was the most basic, and consequently the most inexpensive, of Korg's MS series. Manufactured from 1978 to early 1980, it featured a 32-note (F-C) keyboard and semi-modular design, in that you could reroute the signal of some modules via patch cords. However, you didn't have to use patch cords to make a basic synthesizer sound. A monophonic synth, the MS-10 had one VCO, one VCF, an LFO with multiple waveforms, an ADSR with hold controls, and knobs to control pitch, portamento time, external signal level, resonance, and pulse width. It also had one live performance wheel, for pitch bend. (Excerpted from the A-Z of Analogue Synthesizers, by Peter Forrest, published by Surreal Publishing, Devon, England, and copyright 1994).

Fig. #18: Korg's MS-20 had a brief life, but was the driving force behind the advent of techno music. Image courtesy of Kevin Lightner

MS-10 fans included Aurora, Juan Atkins, Coldcut, Electronic Dream Planet, A Flock of Seagulls, Yuri Gagarin, Stephen Hague, LFO, The Orb, Stereolab, and Youth.

Roland TB-303

The TB-303 (Fig. #19) is a dedicated sequencer/bass-machine originally released by Roland to be paired with the TR-606 drum machine. The idea was to provide an inexpensive substitute for a live drummer and bass player. The TR-606 outsold its bass counterpart by a wide margin, but ironically, the TB-303 is now considered a classic and worth considerably more now than when it was introduced. Bass lines in electronic music are often derived using the Roland TB-303 or the very similar-sounding Rebirth software.

Fig. #19: The TB-303 was designed solely to play programmable bass lines, but ended up being a popular part of acid house and other forms of dance music.

The TB-303 has been part of the sound of 2 Unlimited, 808 State, A Positive Life, Acid Junkies, Acid Rockers, Air Liquide, AlecEmpire, Dave Angel, The Aphex Twin, Apoptygma Berzerk, B.S.E., Barney Arthur, Jeff 'Skunk' Baxter, Beatmasters, The Beloved, Biochip C., Bizarre Inc, Cabaret Voltaire, A Certain Ratio, Coldcut, D.A.V.E., DDR, Dreadzone, The Drummer, Eat Static, Ege Bam Yasi, Electribe 101, Electronic Dream Planet, Frontline

Assembly, Future Sound of London, Laurent Garnier, The Grid, A Guy Called Gerald, Groove Corporation, Haircut 100, Hardfloor, Simon Harris, Richie Hawtin, HIA, Hit Squad, Human League, Marshall Jefferson of DJ Pierre, Guy McAffer, KLF KMFDM, Michael Law, LFO, Chris Liberator, Loaded, The Madness, Man Machine, Massive Attack, Moby, Motiv8, Mulligan, Mushroom of Massive Attack, Nostrum, The Orb, Orbital, The Other two, Ozric Tentacles, Planet 4 Records, Ian Pooley, The Prodigy, Rhythmatic, Tom Robinson, Rowland The Bastard, Sabres of Paradise, Kevi Saunderson, Shades of Rhythm, Insom Shalom, Shamen, Tim Simenon, Sky Cries Mary, Sonic Subjunkies, Squarepusher, Switzerland, Thompson Twins, Mark Tyler, Ultramarine, Ultraviolet, Underground Resistance, and Underworld.
Used by permission: www.synthmuseum.com

SH-101

Known for its fat bass sounds, the Roland SH-101 (Fig. #20) is a monophonic synthesizer, featuring a 2-1/2 octave, 32-note (F-C) keyboard in a light, plastic case. It was designed as a strap-on synth with an optional modulation attachment that stuck out like a guitar neck.

Fig. #20: Designed to cash in on the "strappable keyboard" craze so keyboard players could move up front with guitarists, the SH-101 sold reasonably well but like other vintage Roland gear, has found a new life in dance music.

The SH-101 has been used by Meat Beat Manifesto, Mulligan, Chris Newman, Nitzer Ebb, Nort, Mike Oldfield, OMD, One Dove, William Orbit, Orbital, Ozric Tentacles, Pere Ubu, Primal Scream, The Prodigy, Martin Rex, Rhythmatic, Ian Ritchie, Rowland The Bastard, Sabres of Paradise, Shades of Rhythm, Nigel Shaw, Sheep on Drugs, Tim Simenon of Bomb the Bass, Squarepusher, Stereo MC's, Switzerland, Staja Tanz, Timeshard, Mark Tyler, UB40, Adrian Utley Eric Wilson, bassist of Sublime, Youth, and Zion Train.)
Used by permission The Synthmuseum

As the '80s and '90s progressed, new technologies seemed to explode on to the market place as manufacturers became increasingly more competitive. Perhaps the most significant milestone was the introduction of the digital instrument in the early '80s. Signal processors, keyboards, and drum machines were the first to incorporate the new digital technology; but what really provided the impetus to go digital was the introduction of the Musical Instrument Digital Interface (MIDI), which provided a way to link these new families of instruments together.

What's MIDI?

Traditional musicians had little idea that music, as they had known it, was about to make a radical shift. A concept at first difficult to grasp, the idea of transforming music into digital data was at the very least unusual. The introduction of MIDI, the universal communication platform, enabled digital instruments to talk to each other, and the *sequencer* offered the ability to record a musical performance as a digital arrangement that could play back through an appropriate keyboard or module. Additionally, notes could be shifted and tempos changed without altering the timbre. Suddenly there was a seemingly infinite number of ways the music could be manipulated.

The sequencer found a wide audience, as a performance could be recorded in a number of ways including a method known as *step editing*, where notes were entered one at time rather than played in real time. Step editing meant that you didn't have to be a virtuoso player to achieve a virtuoso performance. This had great appeal, and soon the world seemed to be inundated with MIDI-based music as manufactures clamored to feed the market with a never-ending stream of new products and technologies.

The Digital Keyboard

Along with the sequencer, the digital keyboard became an essential piece of gear for anyone interested in electronic music. Suddenly there was a pivotal shift from the analog keyboard to the algorithm-based digital synthesizer. Instead of controlling sound with big fat knobs and sliders, this new technology relied on internal software that displayed a multitude of editing parameters in small LCD displays mounted on the instrument's surface.

Yamaha DX7

Marking the unofficial dawn of the digital music age, the Yamaha DX7 (manufactured from 1983-1987; see Fig. #21) was an immediate success. Upon its release, it was highly praised and universally sought after as the most advanced synthesizer on the market. Until 1985, no other synth came close to its popularity. A pivotal instrument, the DX7 was simply one of the most important landmarks in synth history. The DX7 not only redefined what a synthesizer sounded like or could do but also redefined the synthesizer market.

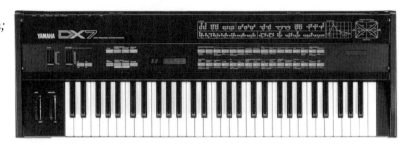

Fig. #21: The DX7 was not only the first mass-market digital synth; it also incorporate innovations such as a pressure-sensitive keyboard, where pressing on a key once it was down could add modulation to the sound, such as vibrato.

Korg M1

The M1 (Fig. #22) was the world's first complete music workstation comprising sampled sounds, a built-in sequencer, and signal processing. A milestone in synthesizer history, the M1 defined the multi-functional approach to music production. The M1 offered 3 different performance modules, including multi, layer, and split sounds, and 100 memory slots for programs and another 100 for combinations of programs. Its multi-mode function allowed assigning up to 8 different programs to different sections of the keyboard, enabling the user to play them as if they were 8 separate synthesizers. Its internal 8-track sequencer stored up to 10 songs and 100 patterns.

Fig. #22: Korg's M1 "workstation" was the synth world's next big hit after DX7 sales started to fade.

Samplers

Early samplers appeared as a "features" in keyboards such as the Ensoniq Mirage. The Mirage, an 8-bit sampling keyboard with 8-voice polyphony, was the first practical sampling keyboard for under $2,000. Sounds were stored using a built-in 3.5 disk drive. In 1985, Akai introduced the S612, which was the first affordable, rack-mounted 12-bit sampler. Although its use of the ill-fated "Quick Disk" storage medium limited sales, Akai went on to become, along with E-mu Systems, one of the world leaders in sampling technology.

Unlike synthesizers, samplers were digital recorders that could record actual audio directly to memory, then store the results in a local hard drive or floppy disk. Once digitized, the sounds could be manipulated and edited much in the same way as MIDI information. Early samplers had very limited memory and somewhat crude sounds due to low sampling rates that restricted high frequency response, and low bit resolutions that resulted in a grainy, coarse (but nonetheless distinctive) sound.

Sampling soon found its way into the DJ world where it was incorporated into mixers that gave the DJ the ability to mix short phrases into the dance mix. Soon samplers started affecting the basic way music was produced, as entire chunks of music could be mixed and edited using the same "cut and paste" methods found in the computer word processing. Today most studios use some form of sampling as a basic tool, and samplers have found their way to almost every style of music.

COMPUTERS AND MUSIC

The Early Days

Early, affordable computers, originally intended for business and writing applications, began finding their way into the home in the late '70s and early '80s. Initially, music software consisted of musical games that produced a series of low-grade beeps. Some software developers began to offer early notation and sight-reading programs. Interestingly enough, the music of this era was decidedly dance-oriented as this was around disco's peak. The relationship between electronic dance music and computers can be traced right back to the beginning.

"In 1976, Stephen Wozniak sold his Volkswagen and Steve Jobs sold his programmable calculator to get enough money to start Apple. In 1977, they introduced the Apple II, a pre-assembled PC with a color monitor, sound, and graphics. It was popular, but everyone knew that a serious computer didn't need any of this...and the Apple II was seen as a toy. Even the Apple name wasn't a serious, corporate sounding name like IBM, Digital Equipment Corporation, or Control data.

"But 1977 also brought competition. The Zilog Z-80 micro-processor, which had been introduced in 1975, was used in the Tandy Radio Shack TRS-80, affectionately called the 'Trash 80.' Apple, Commodore, and Tandy dominated the PC marketplace. The Apple II had 16K bytes of RAM and 16K bytes of ROM; Commodore Business Machines' Personal Electronic Transactor (PET) included 4K RAM and 14K ROM; and the TRS-80 had 4K RAM and 4K ROM.

"In 1980, IBM had started a secret project in Boca Raton, Florida called 'Acorn.' 13 months later, in 1981, IBM introduced the IBM PC, a product that validated the PC as a legitimate business tool. For many people, even those who prided them-selves on being able to operate the "Big Iron," if IBM was making PCs then the small desktop units were worthy of respect.

When the IBM PC hit the market, it was a compete system. Secretly, IBM had provided software developers with prototypes of their PC so they could develop an array of programs that would be available when the machine hit the streets. IBM also developed printers, monitors, and expansion cards for the PC and made it an open system so other manufacturers could develop peripherals for it.

The IBM PC used an Intel 8088 microprocessor, had 16K of RAM, was expandable to 256K, came with on 5.25-inch disk drive and room for a second, and was available with a choice of operating systems: CP/M-86 or IBM PC-DOS, which had been developed by Microsoft.

In 1985 Atari Corporation introduced its new 16-bit computer system called the 520ST (520 stood for the amount of memory in kilobytes, while ST stood for Sixteen/Thirty Two bit processor). Its revolutionary design featured many advance-ments, including MIDI in/out and thru ports. Although IBM,

Macintosh and Amiga gave early music software manufactures a suitable platform for software design, the interfaces and software were awkward and better suited to programmers than musicians.
Jones International Computer Encyclopedia

Embraced by amateurs and professionals, the sleek-looking Atari was truly the first "musician-friendly" computer. It was easier to use and more affordable than the higher priced PCs. Suddenly the average musician was able to hook up a digital synthesizer or drum machine to the computer and run MIDI sequencing software, creating a virtual recording studio. Arrangements could be easily stored on a floppy disk and recalled at a moment's notice. A consummate workhorse, the 520ST represented a major step forward in computer and OS design that is still in use today, years after Atari quit the computer business.

As John Digweed of Bedrock Productions notes, "I use Notator on an Atari. Nick Muir, who I work with, knows the Atari inside out and he does all the programming. [Granted the Atari is considered obsolete]; it's not very fast, but Nick's very fast. William Orbit did most of his mixes on Atari. It's all down to knowing your equipment. You can have the fastest computer in the world, but it's no good unless you know how to use it. When I did the Northern Exposure records with Sasha we used [Digidesign's] Pro Tools for edits and filtering but when we do Remixes, we use the Atari."

The Gear

Remixes can't be produced without gear. As its name implies, electronic music is made with electronic synths, computers, software, and hardware. If you want to be a good remixer, first you need to know how to mix—but make sure you look at all the mixers, computers, samplers, effect processors, hard disk recorders, software, sound cards, and interfaces on the shelves of any good music or DJ shop. At first glance, it boggles the mind. It seems as though there is a new, must-have piece of gear released almost every week. Where will it go from here? To answer this, let's look at what's available now, as well as what might be released in the future through new technologies.

Despite the sea of gear that surrounds us at any given moment, it's actually easy to keep it simple. After all, the idea is to create music, not to get lost in the technology. Initially, learn what the products do and how you might be able to make use of them, but don't get too carried away. It's better to learn one piece of equipment inside and out than to operate banks of gear only adequately. Many schools offer courses and full programs in electronic music and the use of MIDI. Almost anyone can benefit from someone teaching how to use the tools and how to apply them. Whether it's one course at your local community college or at the highly respected Full Sail Recording school in Florida, you can learn some skills that can help you achieve your goals.

To make it easier to understand the different components of remixing, we've broken the gear into basic categories. The objective here is not to cover every piece of gear made for the Remix market—that would take several books. Instead, we'll pick some strategic products based on either historical significance (i.e., older gear that has stood the test of time or has been revived by the Remix market), or because a product embodies the important elements of a product category. We also chose a few pieces just because we use the gear and like it!

As you go through your gear adventures, remember there is no right or wrong setup. Many unique sounds were created because of improperly used equipment. Often you can get more out of the gear that you already own than you can something brand new because you've had more time to learn how to stretch the limits. Keep in mind that the Chemical Brothers, who are technical equipment masters, produced one of their biggest sellers, "Song of the Siren," in their bedroom using an old Akai sampler and an ancient Roland Juno-106 Synth. When it was finished, it was mastered onto a Hitachi VHS Hi-Fi recorder.

TURNTABLES

The turntable has migrated from its antiquated place in the pre-CD consumer world to become the core of the DJ culture. Turntables are commonly found in Remix studios and are often used when assembling samples lifted from old recordings. The birth of hip-hop resurrected old workhorse turntables such as the Technics SL-1200 because of its tougher-than-nails construction and direct drive that could sustain the nightly torture test of "scratching." A staple of the club scene since the early '70s, SL-1200 turntables are the standard in nightclubs around the world.

Technics

The Technics SL-1200 (Fig. #23) direct-drive strobe-monitored turntable was first introduced in 1973, and the near-mythical SL-1200MK2 improved this revolutionary line. Today, Technics offers the SL-1200M3D Direct Drive turntable, which uses the same inner workings as the MK2 but has been further reengineered for smoother nonstop performance.

Fig. #23: The Technics SL-1200 is a standard of the industry.

Numark TT1

The Numark TT1 (Fig. #24) is a new contender that's in the same league as the Technics SL-1200. With a high torque, magnetic direct-drive motor, forward/reverse switch, and 33, 45, 78 rpm speeds, the TT1 will undoubtedly make its mark in the DJ world.

Fig. #24: The Numark TT1 could be the heir apparent to the venerable Technics SL 1200.

DJ MIXERS

Another basic dance necessity is the DJ mixer, which usually consists of two or three channels with phono/line inputs, perhaps some simple EQ, and, of course, a crossfader. This relatively simple device enables the DJ to seamlessly segue from one piece of music to another.

Rane MoJo MM 8z Mixer

The MM 8z features eight stereo inputs. Each of the four assignable buses contains its own three-band EQ, allowing separate equalization for different sources. The four faders are grouped in two pairs, allowing a custom mix of two input sources on each side of the crossfader.

A new feature added to the MM 8z is the two pre/post crossfader assign switches. They allow you to individually assign source 1 or 4 to pre- or post-crossfader. This allows another mixer, drum machine, synth, or wireless mic to be controlled from source 1 or 4, while sources 2 and 3 still use the MM 8z's crossfader. This powerful new feature greatly increases the MM 8z's flexibility, making it one of the most capable mixers in its price range.

Roland DJ-2000 Mixer

The Roland DJ-2000 Professional DJ Mixer gives club DJs more of what they're looking for. It features four-channel mixing with three-band EQ per channel (and two-band EQ for the main mic), intelligent mixer layout, and DJ-friendly features such as an automatic bpm counter, MIDI output for syncing records, and audio CDs with MIDI gear. It also has built-in digital effects (including delay, flanger, slicer, overdrive + delay, overdrive + flanger, auto pan, filter, and "robot voice"). Other features include a dedicated monitor section with assignable cue/sampler output, selectable phono/line inputs and dual mic inputs and level meter. These capabilities make the DJ-2000 ideal not only for traditional club DJs, but also for DJs who want to incorporate MIDI instruments and sophisticated effects processing into their live sets.

American DJ Q-2221/S "Q-DECK"

As an inexpensive alternative to higher-priced DJ mixers, manufacturers such as American DJ, Numark, and Gemini offer a range of affordable models including American DJ's Q-2221/S. The Q-2221/S has two phono inputs, two line inputs, two auxiliary inputs, and one microphone input. The fader allows auto return to preset digital cue points. The Q-Deck also features 100 percent kill buttons for treble, mid, and bass of each channel.

DJ CD PLAYERS

Initially, many predicted that the CD player would ultimately replace vinyl. Although many mobile DJs now prefer the convenience of CDs, the turntable still rules with club DJs. However, CD players are picking up momentum, and many of the new dual CD players feature a built-in mixer.

Numark CDN-34

With 12 seconds of antishock memory and true instant start, the Numark CDN34 provides seamless looping, with an edit function and "stuttering" on-the-fly. With continuous play, beat counter, program play, three-speed forward/reverse and a scanning wheel, the CDN-34 is designed for both live and studio applications.

Pioneer CDJ-700S

The CDJ-700S (Fig. #25) is an extremely compact CD player. You can operate this player just as you can a vinyl turntable by using the jog dial for music search and cue-point selection. Despite its portability, the CDJ-700S is definitely a pro level player.

Fig. #25: The CDJ-700S is known for stuffing pro features in a small box.

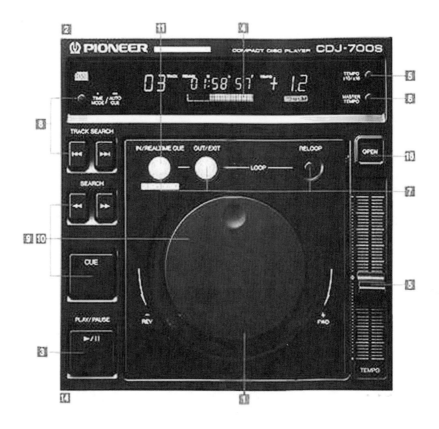

SOUND MODULES

As mentioned in the previous chapter, there are two types of synths: analog and digital. However, the lines are not always that clear-cut, as there are digital emulations of analog synths and analog synths that are controlled via digital circuitry. Each has its advantages and creates different types of sounds, but frankly, all you need to know about a synth can be learned with your ears. If something sounds great, who cares what technology created that sound?

A good but not necessarily expensive synth is essential to producing electronic music. Keep in mind that it's the sound that counts; even a consumer-oriented module may suffice if it has the right stuff. Many can even be triggered via a MIDI keyboard.

Clavia Nord Micro Modular

Used as a staple for dance production, the Clavia's Nord series is made up of modern analog synthesizers. The Nord Micro Modular is a stripped-down and less expensive Nord Modular virtual modular synthesizer, but only with respect to size and polyphony. It can achieve the same "phat" sounds as its more expensive big brothers, including ultra-fat basses, electric FM pianos, inharmonic multisine wave spectra, groovy sequencer bass lines, and more. Also, the Nord Micro Modular is 100 percent patch-compatible with the extensive library developed for the Nord Modular; creating and editing patches is even done using the same PC or Mac editing software as its big brother. When you are satisfied with your patches, you simply save them in the Nord Micro Modular and unhook the PC. Furthermore, the Micro Modular can process external sounds in addition to generating sounds internally.

Roland JP-8080

The new JP-8080 Analog Modeling Synthesizer Module models traditional analog sounds and offers ten-note polyphony. The JP-8080 also offers a unique built-in Voice Modulator (pitch shifting feature) and a SmartMedia card for storing presets (the same mini floppy disk storage platform that can be found in digital cameras). All this is packed in a cool-looking, retro-styled 6U rack-mount module with tons of knobs and sliders for easy sound shaping.

Korg NX5R

In addition to providing proprietary synthesized sounds, the NX5R also includes a tone generator "daughterboard" with sounds specified by Yamaha's XG format. This format provides a standardized palette of sounds, so that those who create MIDI files for XG-compatible machines can be sure that the end results will sound pretty much as intended. (MIDI itself does not associate particular sounds with particular program numbers; program 37 may call up flute on one synthesizer and piano on another. With XG synths, program 37 will always call up the same basic instrument. The General MIDI standard, also called GM, is an earlier specification that does much of the same thing. However, XG not only includes all GM sounds, but many other sounds as well.)

With 96 voices, 48 channel multi-timbrality (i.e., the NX5R can play back a maximum of 48 independent instruments simultaneously), 2365 sounds, and 52 different drum kits, the NX5R provides a wide range of tonal variations in one instrument.

SAMPLERS

The sampler is, in many ways, the heart of Remix and electronic music production. A sampler is a digital recording device that can record sounds via a line or microphone input. In many cases, it can import sounds from floppy disks, CD-ROMs, or computer programs. The sampler also allows you to edit the sample with varying degrees of sophistication and playback. Once recorded, a sample can be played back at different rates to transpose the original recording to the desired pitch, similar to changing the speed on a turntable. In fact, a single sample can be stretched across a keyboard's entire range, although the quality may get iffy with extreme stretching (then again, this can provide some nifty sound mutations that are very useable in Remix applications). Some models include synthesis and sampling in one package. This type of instrument is a good investment for the first-time buyer because it provides an integrated production tool that has more bang for the buck.

Akai

In 1986, the Akai S900 (Fig. #26) became the world's first truly affordable professional multisampler. It became an instant success in Europe. During that time in the U.S., E-mu was the dominant force in samplers, followed by Ensoniq. However, since then, Akai samplers have made considerable inroads into the U.S. market.

Akai's follow-up, the S1000, built further on the S900's reputation and also became a standard, as did subsequent models such as the S1100 and S3000. The latest Akai samplers, the S5000 and S6000, include awesome expansion capabilities and a super-easy user interface that resembles a computer's graphic user interface.

Fig. #26: The Akai S900 started life as a more reasonably priced answer to E-mu's Emulator II, but it acquired a life of its own and took over the European studio scene.

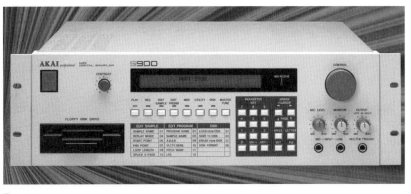

E-mu

Given the cost-effectiveness of today's samplers, it's hard to imagine that the first practical sampler, the Fairlight, cost around $30,000. E-mu brought that price barrier way down with the Emulator I, and the Emulator II, which was listed at the "bargain basement" price of around $8,000, enabled a growing number of studios to get into the sampling act. The E-II was used on many famous recordings of the '80s, including Peter Gabriel's "Shock the Monkey."

Later, an even less expensive model, the Emax, debuted, followed by the Emax II. The Emulator range now spans a variety of models including the Emulator IV. Recent E-mu samplers have acquired a well deserved reputation for cost-effectiveness and excellent sound libraries.

Another landmark E-mu product is the SP-1200, a drum machine that has found tremendous popularity in rap and hip-hop. It started life as the SP-12, graduated to SP-1200 when it added a disk drive, and then eventually went out of production. However, the SP-1200 was so popular in the second-hand market that E-mu relaunched it several years after its demise.

Ensoniq

Ensoniq, now absorbed by E-mu, broke the under-$2,000 price barrier in the mid-'80s with the Mirage. Despite its funky sound quality, it was a major success, and many musicians still use the Mirage for particular sounds that can't be obtained with other samplers. Its follow-ups, the EPS and EPS 16+, achieved even greater success and became a mainstay of R&B groups. Ensoniq's last major sampler introduction, the ASR-10, had an extremely long product life and was favored by many rap artists. Unfortunately, Ensoniq samplers were generally not very expandable, and they are difficult to keep in repair. This makes them less popular in the used sampler market. But for a while there, Ensoniq was every budget-oriented musician's answer to sampling.

Yamaha A3000

Yamaha's first sampler attempt, the TX16W, was a commercial disaster. But what a difference a decade makes! The A3000 is a very impressive and flexible instrument. Designed from the ground up for professional break-beat and phrase sampling, the A3000 (Fig. #27) is intended for use with techno, jungle, hip-hop, and other types of modern dance music. For live use, it includes several control knobs for tweaking sounds in real time. Other features include onboard multieffects and dynamic filters.

Fig. #27: Yamaha's A3000 sampler was designed specifically with modern dance music in mind.

Kurzweil

Kurzweil has always been more of a synthesizer than a sampler company, but their instruments have traditionally included fairly sophisticated sampling and processing functions. While not too common in Remix circles, Kurzweil products, particularly the 2000 and 2500 series, have nonetheless developed quite a cult following over the years. For more information, see the next section on synthesizers.

Roland

Roland had fair success with earlier samplers; the S-760 in particular was popular in Hollywood for soundtrack work. Then, after a fallow period, Roland hit on a winning formula by adapting sampling technology to the new generation of groove-oriented boxes. For example, the SP-202 Dr. Sample is a low-cost sampler that strips away anything that's not needed for DJ-type applications, resulting in a compact, easy-to-use unit optimized for modern dance music. It can calculate bpm from sample length, (it knows that a 500ms phrase works out to 120 bpm) and offers multiple effects (pitch shifter, delay, ring modulation, etc.), different possible sample rates to economize on memory consumption (lower rates use less memory but offer reduced high frequency response), and battery operation with a built-in mic for portability (you can sample your friends, then play back their rants as loops). Total sampling time is over four minutes, expandable to 35 minutes using a 4MB SmartMedia card.

The Scrap Heap of History

Many other companies have introduced samplers over the years. Dynacord, a German company, introduced a fairly competent sampler in the '80s, but the unfavorable exchange rate of the German mark versus the U.S. dollar, along with inadequate documentation, kept it from gaining popularity in the U.S. Casio (yes, the watch people) introduced the first 16-bit resolution sampler, the FZ-10, in the mid-'80s; however, the sound quality was about on a par with the 12-bit Emax, and after an initial flurry of sales, the FZ-10 took a nose dive. Finally, Peavey introduced an excellent rack mount sampler, the Peavey SP, which was way ahead of its time. Designed for expandability and with features still not duplicated in today's gear, the SP suffered from two main problems: a limited sample library of sounds and Peavey's image as a guitar and amp company—people simply didn't think of Peavey as a keyboard manufacturer.

SYNTHESIZERS

If the sampler is the heart of Remix, then the synthesizer is its life's blood. When Kraftwerk began experimenting with hand-made analog synths and vocoded vocals in the '70s, it's likely they had little idea what was to happen as manufactures raced to build better models with more advanced technologies. For a while, it seemed that synthesizers would take over all music, but the market leveled by the mid-'90s as mainstream music turned back to simpler production styles and the acoustic guitars of its roots.

As samplers became more popular, synth makers found themselves struggling to remain relevant. As one solution, manufacturers continued to advance the workstation concept —a workstation being combination of great-sounding synths, effects, and sequencers, sometimes with built-in sampling and SCSI ports to enable a direct connection to SCSI-equipped computers. (All Macs that were released between the Mac Plus and the G3 included SCSI; Windows machines accommodate add-on SCSI boards.) Now, manufacturers are honing their craft with improved, easier-to-use interfaces, better emulation of analog sounds, more comprehensive effects, and often, the ability to read samples or other files in formats used by competing manufacturers.

As modern dance music has progressed, older analog synths and drum machines have been resurrected to become the basis of the new groove sound. Many manufacturers sample (digitally record) vintage keyboards and make them available as digital presets. Through it all, there has been a large, loyal base of keyboard players and producers who carried the synthesizer flag through the lean times. Suddenly, synths are back in style, regaining their rightful place and status as a truly modern instrument. Now, instead of simply using synth sounds to replace real music, we appreciate the amazing and unique sounds that emanate from the modern synthesizer.

It's impossible to give anything more than a cursory overview of synthesizers, but following is an eclectic combination of classic, contemporary, and unique synths of interest to remixers.

Kurzweil

As mentioned earlier, Kurzweil synths are also known for their sampling capabilities. But as synths, Kurzweil has always subscribed to the workstation philosophy, providing sounds, sequencing, and signal processing in one package. They also offer expandability; for example, the K2000VP includes 8MB of sound ROM memory and 2MB of sample RAM, but these are expandable to 24 and 64MB respectively. The sound ROMs are weighted more toward orchestral sounds, but the on-board processing allows for some pretty serious mutating.

Roland

When it comes to synthesizers, Roland is one of the most prolific companies in the world. From legendary, classic synths like the SH-101 and Juno-106 through the D-50 and D-70 synths that combined analog processing with digital waveforms up to the JD-800 with its intensive real-time control options, Roland has always stayed on top of the trends. Current products like the JP-8000 continue the tradition. Although it's a digital synthesizer, the JP-8000 models classic analog sounds with uncanny accuracy—but without the drawbacks, such as tuning instability. Like the classic Roland analog synths of the past, the JP-8000 sports a collection of knobs and sliders for powerful real-time control.

Yamaha

Yamaha has made many synthesizers over the years, but none had the impact of the DX7. The DX7 arguably marked the dawn of the digital music age. Manufactured from 1983 to 1987, the DX7 was an immediate success. Upon its release, it was highly praised and universally sought after as the most advanced synthesizer on the market, and it went on to become one of the most important landmarks in synth history. The DX7 redefined what a synthesizer sounded like and could do; it redefined the synthesizer market.

A major difference of the DX7 compared to previous analog synthesizers was the use of an entirely different synthesis engine, obtainable only with digital electronics and licensed from Stanford University. FM (frequency modulation) synthesis was characterized by clear, bell-like sounds, growling basses, and uncanny imitations of electric pianos and brass instruments. The instrument was difficult to program for most musicians, and this spawned a cottage industry of people who took the time to learn how to program the beast and who offered those patches for sale.

Yamaha rode the FM synthesis wave with subsequent keyboards and rack modules like the TX7, TX81Z, DX7 Mk II, DX100, and the classic TX802, arguably the best implementation of FM synthesis Yamaha ever invented. Eventually, FM synthesis fell out of favor, but it is starting to make a comeback due to its unique sonic qualities.

Korg

Korg also has a few classic instruments under its belt, including the Mono/Poly (which was not really appreciated at the time, but is now a coveted collector's item), the PolySix (the answer to Sequential Circuits' classic Prophet-5), and the Prophecy (a monophonic synth with many classic sounds obtained through digital emulation). Korg's Prophecy not only does an excellent job of making analog sounds, but also uses a process called physical modeling, first introduced in Yamaha synthesizers, which emulates traditional acoustic instruments with a surprising degree of realism.

But Korg's greatest success came with the M1, the world's first complete music workstation comprising sampled sounds, a built-in sequencer, and signal processing. A milestone in synthesizer history, the M1 defined the multifunctional approach to music production. The M1 offered three different performance modules, including multi, layer, and split sounds; 100 memory slots for programs; and another 100 for combinations of programs. Its multimode function allowed you to assign up to eight different programs to different sections of the keyboard, enabling the user to play them as if they were eight separate synthesizers. Its internal 8-track sequencer stored up to ten songs and 100 patterns.

The M1's follow-up, the 01W, was also very successful; Korg's latest instruments, such as the Z1 and Triton, build on the knowledge gained when they created the Prophecy, but they are far more powerful, offering more complex voices, greater polyphony, and more types of synthesis. They are part of a trend in synthesizers to not only provide classic sounds of the past, but to produce new types of sounds possible only with digital technology.

E-mu

Known mostly for their samplers in their early history, E-mu was a company that put a lot of effort into developing sound libraries for their samplers. Eventually, they started putting those samples into ROM form and creating synthesizers; the first of these, the Proteus, offered a large number of voices and multitimbral operation for under $1,000, shattering the price-performance ratio of the time. Knowing a good thing when they saw one, E-mu spun off numerous other rack mounts, including the Orbit (designed specifically for dance music), Planet Phatt (intended for rap), and Carnival (specializing in Latin music). Most of these modules, as well as the more advanced Audity 2000, are still available today and are widely in use.

The European Contingent

Europeans were the first to resurrect the synthesizer from stasis, with a great example being Clavia's Nord Lead. This Swedish synth, released in 1995, immediately became a groundbreaking success as the world's first virtual analog synthesizer. It used a completely new synthesis concept: real-time digital emulation of analog synthesis—no samples at all!

With the release of the Nord Lead, a new industry standard was born. Musicians around the world praised its warm analog sound, operational simplicity, and smart industrial design. Two years later, the Nord Lead was followed by Nord Lead 2, which brought the virtual analog concept even further, adding a number of improvements and new features.

Other European manufacturers include Waldorf (whose Wave and Q synthesizers, although pricey, are coveted by those seeking the ultimate in analog simulation) and dance-oriented synths by companies like Novation and Quasimidi.

EFFECTS PROCESSORS

Effects have always played an important role in the development of modern dance music. remixers and producers apply radical filtering, delay, reverb, and flanging effects to add exciting elements to a track. King Tubby (Fig. #28), the legendary pioneer of dub, was an electrical engineer from Jamaica who built custom reverbs and other effects for his studio where he created specialized dance hall remixes (dubs) of popular tracks of the day. His influence is still felt today, as DJs and remixers are constantly looking for anything that will give their track an added edge.

Fig. #28: King Tubby is the legendary pioneer of the dub style of remixing.

Older, analog effects, such as those made by Electro-Harmonix, MXR, DOD, and others are sought after for their real-time playability. Digital multieffects are not quite as well-suited to the task, owing to their more limited interfaces; however, many of these allow for MIDI control of various parameters. This means you can use MIDI foot pedals or fader boxes (like the Peavey PC-1600) to vary parameter values in real time.

With the increasing Remix market, though, manufacturers are now producing boxes with old-school interfaces but state-of-the-art digital technology. As there are even more signal processors than synths, we won't try to be complete, and will instead concentrate on a few of unique offerings intended solely for dance and Remix music.

Electrix

A newcomer to the world of Remix, production, and live DJs, Electrix (Fig. #29) offers performance effects such as the Filter-Factory, WarpFactory and Mo-FX, along with their new MoDs line, which are designed for live as well as studio applications.

Fig. #29: Their unique packaging design allows the Electrix processors to be used as tabletop or rack-mount devices.

Each product has custom nonslip knobs, a switchable power supply for different countries, large back-lit buttons, and MIDI in/out/thru, so real-time performances can be recorded as MIDI events into a sequencer. A phono preamp allows you to connect a turntable directly into an Electrix processor, so effects can be cued without using up your mixer's auxiliary sends. Analog I/O, using 1/4-inch stereo jacks, is also included for studio applications.

WarpFactory

WarpFactory is a vocoder for DJs, engineers, and musicians. A vocoder superimposes the characteristics of one instrument onto another; for example, using voice to modulate guitar or keyboards to create talking instrument effects. However, sources other than voice can be used, such as drums modulating bass. Additional controls can modify the sound in real-time.

FilterFactory

FilterFactory is a performance-oriented resonant filter bank designed specifically for DJs and remixers. It can add filter sweeps and modulation effects to records, CDs, keyboards, etc. Perhaps most importantly, modulation can be synched manually to the rhythm (using a tap tempo button) or automatically by following the MIDI clock rate.

Mo-FX

Mo-FX is a live performance–oriented, multieffects processor that emphasizes real-time control and playability of the effects. The Mo-FX contains four FX modules: distortion, flange, auto-pan/tremolo, and delay effects. Flange, tremolo, and delay effects can sync to the rhythm via tap tempo or MIDI clock.

Red Sound Federation Pro

Red Sounds' Federation Pro is another example of a quality, performance-oriented, bpm-savvy effects unit. It includes several effects that can be synchronized to the tempo via a "beat extraction" engine; this analyzes incoming audio, derives the tempo, then syncs effects to this tempo according to user-selected timing presets (quarter note, triplet, whole note, etc.). The effects are:

Filter/LFO—A resonant analog filter section that features familiar controls for frequency, resonance, and envelope modulation and allows LFO modulation that syncs to the tempo.

Flanger—Similar to the filter, but it sweeps using time delay rather than filtering effects.

Cutter/Volumer—A dual-function cutter section that can either "gate" the audio signal to produce dramatic chopping effects, or "swell" (ramp up) the audio volume using a rising sawtooth shape for softer, more pulsing effects (similar to rapidly moving a level fader).

Delay—Provides up to 1.5 seconds of delay and a "repro" control that can morph the delayed signal quality from clean through vintage tape machine to "grunge" echo reproduction. The speed control models the performance of a vintage tape echo machine by glitchlessly changing the delayed signal's pitch and rate.

Panning—Features a "spatial panning system" that splits the audio signal into low, mid, and high frequencies. The separated frequencies are then panned across the stereo field in opposing directions or a "chasing" pattern to produce 3D-type effects.

Korg Kaoss Pad

The Korg Kaoss Pad (Fig. #30) lets you control effects with the touch of a finger using an "X-Y" pad. The X-Y pad provides separate MIDI controller outputs for both horizontal or vertical finger motions (or "draw" diagonally to send both at once). For example, you can simultaneously control a delay line's delay time and the feedback, or a filter's cutoff and resonance. The X-Y pad can also be scraped or tapped (struck lightly) to control the effect sound, allowing "switch-type" effects that are impossible to create with knobs or sliders.

Sixty effects programs include time-based effects such as delay, reverb, and pitch shifter; filtering; and modulation-type effects such as flanger, phaser, and pan. You can also press a Hold switch to freeze the effect setting at the current location of the X-Y pad.

Fig. #30: The Korg Kaoss pad is an affordable and easy to use real-time effects processor.

Groove boxes, a term coined by Roland, has become a universally accepted name for equipment that is aimed at the Remix and production markets. Judging by the wave of new products that are being released by many manufacturers, remixers of the future will not be lacking for gear.

Groove boxes are usually housed in tabletop-style packaging and combine tone generation, an easy-to-use sequencer, effects, and plenty of cool presets. They don't usually include a traditional keyboard, but instead offer large pads that can be bashed on for drum sounds. Like the keyboard workstations of the '80s, groove boxes take an all-in-one approach that tries to put as much functionality as possible into a single box. They are a great way to get into remixing, especially if you have somewhat limited technological chops and/or budget.

Following are some representative groove boxes.

Akai MPC60
In 1987, the MPC60 production center integrated a sampler, drum machine, and MIDI sequencer into a compact, tabletop-type package. Because of the ease with which you could create grooves—no need to boot up a computer or get different pieces of gear to talk to each other—the MPC60 became an instant success in the rap and hip-hop fields.

Akai MP2000XL
The MPC2000XL (Fig. #31) is the latest generation of the sampler/drum machine/MIDI sequencer product line that began with the MPC60. It incorporates such esoteric (but useful) features as time stretching, resampling, track mute keys, simultaneous playback of a second sequence, and a folder-based file management scheme similar to the type used in personal computers. Also, much effort was expended on simplifying and improving the user interface to make the MPC2000XL better-suited to live performance.

Fig. #31: Akai's MPC2000XL continues the groove box tradition started by the MPC60 and, before that, the Linn 9000.

E-mu/Ensoniq ASR-X Pro

The ASR-X Pro (Fig. #32) incorporates sampling, resampling, 16-track sequencing, synthesis, and sophisticated effects. It includes a standard SCSI interface for easy integration with other SCSI-based devices (such as computers, CD-ROM drives, etc.), expandability to 66MB of sample RAM, and a wealth of on-board sounds that can be expanded with additional hardware sound boards. Like the MPC-family devices, you trigger its sounds with large, easy-to-hit pads rather than a keyboard.

Fig. #32: The ASR-X Pro's tabletop format makes it ideal for live use as well as studio applications.

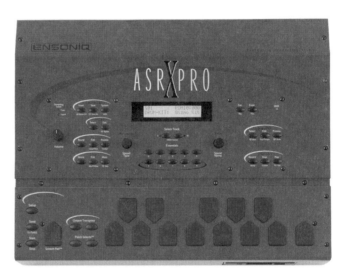

The ASR-X Pro is also compatible with sample libraries developed for the Ensoniq ASR-10 and EPS and can import samples from Akai S1000/1100 and Roland sound libraries.

Roland MC 505

The MC-505 is a self-contained, retro-styled dance music sequencer and sound module with several unique features. The most striking one is the D-Beam controller, an infrared-based controller that responds to hand movements—that's right, wave your hands in the air and change the sound! Other cool features include three independent, synchronizable effects processors; onboard arpeggiator; multiple outputs (three stereo/six mono); and a slot that accepts external 2MB and 4MB SmartMedia cards to store patterns and patches, as well as provide direct pattern playback.

Yamaha RM1x

The Yamaha RM1x is a fairly standard groove box: tone generator, sequencer, MIDI compatibility, etc. However, it has an outstanding user interface that makes it easy to create and edit patterns on-the-fly; there's also a large keyboard, several real-time controller knobs, and dedicated buttons to mute and unmute tracks during playback. It's also possible to make very fine adjustments to notes, such as note offset, clock shift, gate offset, and velocity offset.

Korg-Electribe

The Electribe boxes feature tone generation along with banks of programmable or preset grooves. They are extremely compact. There are two different models that share similar packaging.

The Electribe R is designed for creating rhythms; its main claim to fame is that the drum sounds borrow from the sound modeling engines used in the Korg Prophecy and Korg Z1, two high-end keyboards known for their analog emulations. It also includes standard sampled sounds such as crash, open hi-hat, closed hi-hat, and handclaps.

The built-in step sequencer has 16 pad keys, but the coolest part is that each pad key lights up so you can easily see the rhythm a particular part is programmed to play. There are also 12 trigger pads for triggering sounds in real time.

The Electribe A specializes in modeled analog synthesizer sounds, with lots of real-time programming controls. Like the Electribe R, there are 16 pad keys that light up to show the pattern being played; these can also be used to play pitched notes just like a standard keyboard.

Analog and digital recorders are another good way to produce or remix electronic music tracks. By layering one track on top of another, creative producers and remixers are able to build a full production piece by piece. The portable studio concept combines a mixing board with multitrack recording capability. Usually offered as 4- and 8-track models, the idea of a multifunctional tool is very attractive to those on a limited budget.

Manufacturers offer a variety of recording formats that range from analog and digital tape to minidisc (both 4- and 8-track multitrack minidisc recorders are available). Analog, cassette-based 4-track portastudios are priced quite reasonably and are a great way to work out ideas and listen to live mixes. Digital models can create high quality recordings suitable for release.

Again, we can't provide a comprehensive guide, but following are some representative examples.

TASCAM
424mkIII
A 4-track recorder with an 8-input mixer, the TASCAM 424mkIII recorder features four mic/line input channels with several different types of inputs: XLR (mic level), high impedance (for guitar), and two standard stereo inputs. With two effect sends, 2-band EQ, dbx noise reduction, and 3.75 ips (inches per second) tape speed—twice that of standard cassettes—the 424mkIII offers reasonably high quality at an affordable price.

414mkII
The 414mkII Portastudio, marketed as a cost-effective "sketchpad," offers a high-speed transport, high and low EQ, and dbx noise reduction, which means great sound. For convenience, there are also two XLR mic inputs and a 1/4-inch high-impedance guitar input.

Fostex DMT-8VL
The DMT-8VL is an entry-level hard disk recording-based system. Unlike some systems that use data compression to squeeze more data onto a hard disk (and possibly compromise audio quality in the process), the DMT-8VL uses no form of data compression and thus retains as much of the original sound quality as possible.

There are eight full-function channel inputs; the first two handle both microphone and line signals. All channels have 2-band shelving EQ, along with two auxiliary sends per channel (this makes it easy to add outboard effects and signal processing). The in-line monitor design minimizes repatching, and makes track layering a virtually painless process.

Unlike tape recording, after recording your tracks to disk, you can cut, copy, paste, and move audio within a track or across different tracks to build a "perfect" multitrack master. Another feature you won't find on tape is the undo control—if you record on the wrong track by accident, no problem.

Alesis Studio Pack
Alesis, a leader in digital tape recording, currently offers the Alesis ADAT StudioPack, a reasonably-priced, all-in-one recording studio setup that offers the tools needed for digital recording, mixing, effects, and dynamics processing. The ADAT StudioPack even includes interconnection cables, as well as an instructional video that offers helpful advice in setting up the studio and taking advantage of its capabilities.

The package's centerpiece is the ADAT-LX20, a 20-bit, 8-track digital tape recorder. The LX20 is compatible with tapes produced on any ADAT, from the original 16-bit version introduced in 1991 to the top-of-the-line M20. With well over 100,000 ADATs in use around the world, many musicians collaborate by exchanging ADAT tapes.

The Studio 24 recording console offers in-line monitoring, so eight channels can be monitored and sent to tape at the same time without repatching your cable setup. For processing, the NanoVerb is an easy-to-use signal processing that can add reverb, delay, chorus, flange, multieffects and other effects to your mixes. The NanoCompressor completes the StudioPack with its effective dynamics processing and limiting. Combined, this system is the basis of a pro-level studio at an affordable price.

Roland VS-1680
Roland took the portable studio concept to new levels with the VS-880, one of the most popular self-contained, hard disk recorders ever made. The latest addition to the product line, the VS-1680 (Fig. #33), is a 16-track, digital audio workstation that

can record in resolutions up to 24 bits, as well as provide editing, mixing, and effects processing in a compact, tabletop workstation.

The 16-track figure is somewhat misleading, as the VS-1680 allows up to 16 *virtual* tracks per physical track. For example, you can record 16 tracks of a guitar solo, select just the best bits, and mix them down to a single physical track. The digital mixer provides 26 channels of fully automated digital mixing. Other features include: a huge graphic LCD, optional stereo multieffects processors, ten audio inputs (two balanced XLR mic inputs with phantom power, six balanced 1/4-inch inputs, and one stereo digital input), 12 audio outputs (eight RCA-type audio outputs, two stereo digital outputs, and headphones out), and direct audio CD recording and data backup using the optional VS-CDR-16 CD recorder (or VS-CDR-S2 CD recorder with System Expansion). The digital ins and outs accept either coaxial or optical signals.

Fig. #33: Roland VS-1680

MUSIC SOFTWARE

Music software encompasses myriad programs that enable almost any computer to interact with digital instruments. Using a MIDI interface, most computers can easily create music when connected to external MIDI-compatible sound modules, keyboards, samplers, and drum machines. However, many computers now include sound cards with built-in synthesizers, so sometimes it's possible to create music solely in the computer, with no external devices at all.

Let's look at some typical music software categories.

Remix: The Electronic Music Explosion

Sequencers

Sequencers record MIDI data and then play it back into MIDI-compatible devices. While the data is in the computer, it can be edited. For example, anything from a single note to an entire passage of notes can be shortened, lengthened, transposed, deleted, moved, copied, or transformed in many other ways. Another common editing function, quantization, can correct timing inaccuracies by moving an off-beat note closer to the beat. Sequencers often include the ability to print out scores and/or edit using standard notation as well as other graphic approaches, such as the piano roll type of display (Fig. #34).

Fig. #34: The piano roll display. The position of a rectangle indicates the note's pitch (higher on the screen means higher pitch), while the length indicates the note duration.

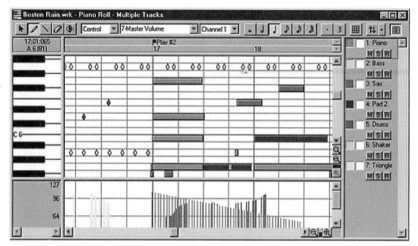

Sequencing software has become an essential tool for many songwriters, composers, remixers, and producers as it allows music to be played on a controller in real-time or by step editing (i.e., off-line, nonreal-time note entry). The computer records and plays a performance back precisely the way it was played. Sequencing software lets you record different performances of different instruments at different times and hear it all play back simultaneously. For example, you could record a drum track, add a bass part, and then later record a synth line while listening to any combination of the previously recorded parts.

Digital Audio Editors

These programs allow editing digital audio, such as making passages softer, louder, applying various effects, adding equalization, cutting, pasting, and the like. Editing programs can even perform seemingly magical tricks like removing hum from a noisy signal or clicks and pops from a record. Most digital audio editors are designed to work on two tracks at a time. They also can convert among various file formats. For example, you might want to save a song file as an MP3-format file suitable for uploading to a website or to e-mail to a friend.

Digital Audio Multitrack Recorders

Multitrack digital audio recorders are essentially "virtual" tape recorders that record to hard disk instead of tape. They frequently include editing functions (although the roster may not be as "deep" as programs optimized for digital audio editing), as well as a virtual mixing console for doing your mix. This will generally include automated mixing functions, so you needn't move the onscreen faders whenever you want to make changes, as you would with a traditional hardware mixer. Instead, you program the changes you want, store them, and move on to the next sound.

MIDI + Digital Audio Sequencers/Recorders

This type of software incorporates both MIDI sequencing and digital audio recording, allowing you to work with both types of tracks side-by-side. They require a powerful computer because you're asking it to do a lot, but they are amazingly flexible and are the recording medium of choice for many electronic musicians. Most modern sequencers can record, edit, and play back both MIDI and digital audio.

MP3 Players and Jukeboxes

Files encoded in the MP3 file format have become a very popular method of recording and listening to near-CD quality stereo tracks, as they can be easily downloaded from the Internet. MP3 players allow you to play back MP3 files over your computer's audio connections (e.g., a sound card); MP3 jukeboxes can arrange files in a particular playing order, allowing for hours of uninterrupted music at a time.

For Remix fans, perhaps the most significant piece of MP3-related software is the PC DJ program from VisioSonic. This software sets up two virtual turntables onscreen and lets you cue up, play back, and beat-match MP3 files stored on your hard drive. The program can also "rip" tracks from your CD collection and convert them to MP3. The best part about all this, of course, is you don't have to lug a huge record collection to the gig—just bring a laptop with a big hard drive (to store all your song files), and run the PC DJ software. As with many types of software, you can download a demo version of the program from their website.

Educational Software

If you want to learn an instrument, train your ear, learn harmony theory, or just about anything else involving music education, suitable software is available.

Software Synthesizers

Computers are great at crunching numbers, and sounds can be represented mathematically, so it has always made sense to use computers as sound generators. However, until only a few years ago, mainstream computers didn't have the power necessary to do this in real time. There are stories of composers in the '60s who programmed sounds on punch cards and had to wait a day or more for the computer to process the data and output a sound—which might then last only a few seconds! We've come a long, long way since then; even low-cost computers can generate dozens of complex voices, all under MIDI control.

Algorithmic Composition

Sometimes called *auto-accompaniment* software, these programs create music all by themselves, often based on parameters you input (tempo, key, chord progression, etc.). Some of these, like Band-in-a-Box and the Jammer, provide remarkably musical results. They can't take off on amazing flights of fancy, but they work well with specific styles keyed to a specific context. Musicians often use these programs to create backing tracks and then overdub real lead lines themselves.

Plug-ins

Plug-ins are accessory programs designed to run in conjunction with a host program. For example, noise reduction programs are fairly large and complicated and are not needed by everyone. Therefore, a manufacturer who makes a digital audio editing program might not include noise reduction in the basic package but will offer it as a plug-in. That way, those who need the function can pay for it, and those who don't need it don't have to.

Let's look at some typical programs from the above categories. Again, this is not meant to be an exhaustive treatment, but it will give you an idea of the types of programs that are available.

Multitrack Recorders

Steinberg Cubase VST (Mac/Windows)

Cubase VST is a MIDI + digital audio program that pioneered the use of "native" processing (i.e., using the computer to do effects like reverb and compression instead of relying on outboard, hardware-based units). Originally written for the Atari, Cubase has long dominated the European Remix scene due to the Atari's popularity there. As the Atari started to fade, Cubase was rewritten first for the Mac, then for the Windows platform; a BeOS-compatible version is rumored to be in development.

A standard sound card is all that's needed to take advantage of the audio features of Cubase, although more sophisticated sound cards (such as those with multiple channels) provide correspondingly more flexibility. Steinberg also set two important standards: the VST (and now the VST 2.0) standard for plug-ins and ASIO, a method that promotes multichannel operation while reducing computer-induced latency (delay).

Emagic Logic Audio (Mac/Windows)

Like Steinberg, Emagic is a German company that was heavily involved in the Atari during its heyday. Logic Audio is functionally similar to Cubase VST and is even compatible with the VST and ASIO specifications. In fact, both Cubase and Logic have been around for so long and have undergone so many revisions that they have more similarities than differences. The reason you might choose one over the other is more a personal preference of style and working habits than it is any overwhelming technological advantage one program has over the other.

Cakewalk Pro Audio (Windows)

Years ago, when Greg Hendershott released the first Cakewalk MIDI sequencer for DOS, most enthusiasts predicted its downfall because it was designed for a computer known primarily for business applications. Well, those people were wrong—when the PC started taking off for music applications, Cakewalk was already well-entrenched. Cakewalk Pro Audio (Fig. #35) combines MIDI and digital audio and accepts plug-ins for both digital audio and MIDI. Recently, Cakewalk teamed with Peavey Electronics, who produced a companion hardware box with moving faders that allows for true, hands-on automated mixing. This is far more convenient than using a mouse to painstakingly adjust onscreen faders one at a time.

Fig. #35: Cakewalk's Pro Audio software, a MIDI sequencing and pro audio package

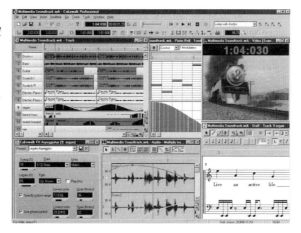

Opcode StudioVision (Mac)

StudioVision was the first program to integrate MIDI sequencing and digital audio recording software and the first to include audio-to-MIDI/MIDI-to-audio conversion. The latter allows you convert a monophonic piece of digital audio (e.g., a flute part or vocal) into MIDI data with a reasonably high degree of accuracy, which can then drive synthesized voices. Even cooler, though, is if you edit the MIDI data (e.g., change level, add vibrato, etc.), those changes are applied to the digital audio used to create the MIDI data.

Digidesign Pro Tools (Mac/Windows NT)

While there are several digital audio workstations on the market today, Pro Tools can truly be called the professional's program. It's used to produce chart-topping music (Ricky Martin's "La Vida Loca," for example) and to create film soundtracks and special effects that contribute to box office smashes like *The Phantom Menace* and *Titanic*. Except for the stripped-down free Pro Tools LE version, this program costs a bundle. In addition, plug-ins for Pro Tools tend to be more costly than plug-ins for programs such as Cubase and Logic. Hardware interfaces are also available, which also aren't cheap. But for many Pro Tools users, it would take nothing less than a commandment from God to get them to switch to something else.

PG Music PowerTracks Pro Audio 5 (Windows)

Surprisingly inexpensive, PowerTracks Pro Audio is a capable digital audio MIDI workstation with features well suited to musicians, students, and songwriters. With integrated digital audio/MIDI recording and built-in music notation, PowerTracks turns even basic Windows-compatible sound cards into the basis of a quality recording studio. A great bang for the buck.

Mark of the Unicorn (MOTU) Digital Performer (Mac)

Long a mainstay on the Macintosh, Digital Performer allows you to simultaneously record and play back multiple tracks of digital audio and MIDI data in a totally integrated, creative environment. It provides the capabilities of a multitrack digital recording system, automated digital mixer, reverb, effects, EQ, and compression. A recent MOTU development, MTS (MIDI Time Stamping) currently provides the best MIDI timing accuracy on the market.

Loop-Based Auto Performance Programs

A loop is a digital recording that is usually relatively short (one or two measures) and is designed to play back continuously—in other words, when playback reaches the end of the file, it immediately jumps back to the beginning. The loop, whether it's an individual drum pattern or a fully produced groove, is often the basis of an electronic production. Additional loops can be added to the mix to layer the production, building or breaking down as the piece develops. Some manufactures have recognized that building loops from scratch is a tedious process, particularly because of the difficulty of matching loops of different keys or tempos. Consequently, they've developed programs that will automatically adjust the timing of different loops to create a homogeneous rhythm.

Sonic Foundry Acid Pro (Windows)

Acid Pro is an amazingly easy to use and powerful program that can beat match loops of different tempos, as well as change pitch for loops in different keys. It stores most loops in RAM, allowing for huge numbers of tracks limited only by computer memory, but it can also record and play back a limited number of hard disk tracks.

Acid allows you to preview any loop before adding it to your mix, automatically matching the tempo and key in real time. Adding or deleting loops is as simple as clicking and dragging; volume, pan, and effects envelopes are available for each track to create automated mixes. Acid also accepts plug-ins that follow the DirectX protocol proposed by Microsoft. Sonic Foundry also offers a large number of loop libraries with prerecorded loops ready to use in Acid. In fact, Acid is such a cool program for remixing that many a Mac addict has ended up buying a PC or PC emulation software solely in order to run it.

Steinberg Recycle (Windows/Mac)

Recycle is an audio processing tool for drum loops and grooves. It uses a technique known as "slicing" to divide the loop into individual segments. Once the sample has been sliced, the individual segments are transmitted to your sampler and mapped to the keyboard. By driving the keyboard with a sequencer, you can speed up or slow down the tempo of the loop without affecting the fidelity. Alternatively, you can use Recycle directly with Cubase VST, obviating the need for an external sampler.

IK Multimedia Groove Maker (Windows/Mac)

Now distributed in the U.S. by Cakewalk and incorporating a large loop library, Groovemaker allows just about anyone to produce professional music tracks in minutes. Random combination technology allows users to surf literally millions of groove combinations on-the-fly without stopping the music. With just a few clicks, tons of professional-sounding, royalty-free tracks are ready to be exported for music or multimedia use.

Mixman Studio (Windows/Mac)

Mixman Studio's remixing features allow arranging digital audio to enhance a musical composition or create entirely new works by combining audio samples using WAV files or files in Mixman's TRK format. Mixman Studio was designed to deliver professional remixing capabilities to anyone with a passion or interest in music without sacrificing audio quality. It greatly simplifies the beat-matching process.

Mixman Studio 1.5 is real-time music performance software that gives Sound Blaster Live! users the ability to remix up to 16 tracks of digital audio with control over pitch, tempo, and beat. In addition to the TRK and WAV formats, Mixman Studio also supports Creative Technology's SoundFont technology.

Software Synthesizers

If you own a computer but don't have a synthesizer, don't despair! Software developers have been very busy creating programs that will generate very believable sounds using your computer's internal sound card. Now you can easily create drum sounds, bass lines, and numerous synthesizer sounds using these new hybrid wonders.

Steinberg Rebirth (Windows/Mac)

A fully automated software synth program, Rebirth features four pieces of classic music hardware reincarnated as software. Emulating distinctive analog sounds, Rebirth includes two 303 bass lines along with 808 and 909 rhythm sections that include digital delay, distortion, and compression integrated with a fully automatic sequencer. Rebirth is an easy-to-use, self-contained software synthesizer that needs no external synthesizers, samplers, or special sound cards.

D-Lusion Rubber Duck (Windows)

RubberDuck H30+ is a real-time software synthesizer dedicated to electronic dance music. Roughly based on the well-known Roland TB-303, the RD H30+ synthesis model consists of an oscillator wave with a resonant filter sweep applied to it combined with a simple hardware sequencer design that creates the typical twisted, screaming, bubbling bass sound that is often used in acid house, goa trance, or techno productions.

D-Lusion DrumStation (Windows)

DrumStation DT-010 is an easy-to-use software drum computer based on the sounds of the legendary Roland drum computers TR-909, TR-808, and TR-606. The program combines cool vintage drum machine sounds with cutting-edge MIDI technology.

Koblo Vibra 9000 and Vibra 7000 (Mac)

The Vibra 9000 is a true stereo software synth, with two oscillators, three envelopes, six selectable filters, two LFOs, an extensive modulation matrix, and an arpeggiator. You can save and load presets on-the-fly, export your parts to a Sound Designer II file to load into your sampler or multitrack recorder, and control pretty much everything via MIDI. The Vibra 7000 (included with the Vibra 9000) is a mono version of the 9000, requiring only half the DSP horsepower. Both synths display every parameter onscreen, and you can twist and turn anything on the screen via the mouse or MIDI and get immediate feedback, just as could with an old analog monster.

Digital Audio Editing Programs

Most samplers were developed as stand-alone hardware boxes. Many remixers and producers spend days at a time bent over these boxes straining to read small LCD screens. In time, software developers began to release visually oriented packages that let users see the WAV files clearly for easy editing.

Syntrillium Cool Edit Pro (Windows)

Cool Edit Pro is a digital audio recorder, editor, and mixer for Windows. Based on Cool Edit 96 (Syntrillium's award-winning shareware application), Cool Edit Pro is easy to learn and use. It includes a full arsenal of digital effects and can mix up to 64 tracks using just about any sound card.

Sonic Foundry Sound Forge (Windows)

Sound Forge 4.5 is professional, intuitive sound editing software for Windows that includes an extensive set of audio processing tools and effects for manipulating audio. In addition to opening MPEG-1 Layer 3 (MP3) files, Sound Forge 4.5c now saves in this format. Other features include batch processing, spectrum analysis, digital effects, and the ability to run with DirectX plug-ins. Sound Forge 4.5 also supports Windows Media Technologies 4.0, a new streaming media protocol from Microsoft that features an advanced approach to digital content delivery.

CHAPTER 4

Takin' It to the Streets

DEVELOPING YOUR OWN SOUND

So with everyone and his dog trying to get into the biz, how do you make your own mark? If you're just starting out it's important to listen and begin to understand the nuances in the multitude of dance styles. Whether you're into drum and bass, hip-hop or deep house, learn to know the subtle differences between the genres. Modern dance production liberally borrows from every type of music imaginable. Learn to do the same.

If you have educated yourself about the many types of music around the world, identify what turns you on. Be influenced by others but don't copy what they're doing. If you spin records, constantly be on the look out for unique and obscure vinyl. Work unusual recordings into your set and let them serve as a signature of your sound. It may be that every style of music has already been done but you can still offer your own unique interpretations.

If you are producing music, use your sampler in creative ways. There are thousands of sample CDs on the market that can help you to build a groove but don't become too reliant on them. Take a tape recorder with you to into the street to capture the endless variety of sounds that occur in everyday life. Bring these sounds back to your studio and get to work editing and creating that perfect loop which could set you apart from the rest.

DEVELOPING A LOCAL FOLLOWING

DJs who achieve local club nights don't get there by accident. Most likely they have spent countless hours practicing and playing parties for free. You'll never know how your music will affect a crowd until you present it to a new audience. Play anywhere and everywhere that you can. Pay attention to the crowd and learn to play to the mood of the moment. Almost every experienced DJ will recommend that you not use planned sets as they are not flexible enough to suit everyone. Each night is different and the mood of a room can change drastically in a matter of minutes. Learn to be in tune with a crowd and to provide the right music for the right moment. Above all, be serious about what you're doing. If you are providing entertainment, you're on the job so keep a clear mind and try to avoid substances that hinder your instincts and creativity.

If you have a computer, develop a mailing list and use it religiously. An easy way to start is to take a spiral notebook with you to every gig. Get everyone you can to sign the book including email, address and phone number. Once you have started a list, create a database from the names and let them know when you are playing next well in advance. Another good way to communicate is to create your own electronic newsletter to keep fans up to date. Despite his world-class status, I still get weekly email from John Digweed who religiously promotes his new record releases and gigs using email to a worldwide audience. John even includes directions via London's famed tube to his weekly *Bedrock Club night*.

NETWORKING

Many times in life it's not what you know but *who* you know. This old adage is particularly true with dance culture and the networking you do today could be the break you've been looking for tomorrow. Don't be afraid to talk to DJs, remixers, and producers. Often you'll find that they are very approachable and are willing to listen to what you have to say. Don't forget, even if they are on top at the moment, they've been in your shoes before and might be able to offer valuable advice.

A great way to make connections is by attending trade shows that are held frequently in many areas across the country. The biggest North American dance schmooze festival is the *Miami Music Conference* held every spring in Florida. Producers, remixers and DJs from around the globe gather for a week-long party and conference that offers seminars and workshops during the day in addition to the many club showcases at night. Other popular trade shows include the DJ Expo held in August in Atlantic City and in March in San Francisco. Chicago, Atlanta, Texas and other areas offer regional shows that provide great opportunities to make connections that can help you along with your career. Check around; there is likely to be one near you.

If you go to one of these conventions, use your time wisely. Don't stay out so late that you sleep through the day's activities. Be prepared with business cards and demo tapes but don't automatically thrust a tape on someone without developing a rapport with the person. Sometimes, a brief conversation is better. Be business like, ask if your potential contact is willing to accept a demo from you first. If they are open to this, get a mailing address and send them a tape or a CD with a professional cover letter when you get home. Remember, it's business – the more professionally you can present yourself, the more likely you are to succeed.

Presentation is everything. You can design your own custom labels or get a friend to help. Create an image that somehow suits you and the music you are presenting. It's great if you can burn your own CD but cassettes work as well. Much of our lives are spent in a car and a good cassette mix can find its way to the right person who may listen to you while driving. Above all follow this basic rule: make sure that your name, telephone number and address is clearly marked on the case *and* the CD or cassette itself. You would be amazed how many people forget to do this. All the great material in the world won't get you anywhere if the listener does not have a contact number.

SELF-PROMOTION

Self-promotion is crucial to your survival. Many established DJs and producers started out as promoters and learned the inner workings of the industry. Get to know the local promoters in your area. You might be able to convince them to put you on the same bill as a big name artist. Save every flyer, ad or write up that you are involved with in a scrapbook. This may serve you well down the road as a portfolio of your past achievements and could help to get you work in the future.

You can also try you own hand at promotion by banding together with other like minded artists to promote your own party. But be careful! You can lose your shirt in a hurry if you take on too much to begin with. If you have a legitimate venue, work with the owner to insure that all the regulations are in place. It's important to know the details of fire codes and local bylaws. Work with the police! Believe it or not, your friends in blue might be your best allies when it comes to promoting an event. You'd be surprised how helpful many cops can be if you work with them from the beginning. If you're new to the game start out small. It's better to have a small success than a big bust.

Parties come from an underground tradition and are still usually promoted by word of mouth and of course, the handbill style flyer. These flyers often have a theme and wild graphics that create the right image. Seek out young artists who are looking to break into the graphic business. They may help you to create a great flyer without costing an arm and a leg. Working with the right person can make your promotion a success. After all, dance culture is about look, feel and sound.

AN INTERVIEW WITH DAVE JURMAN

Senior Director of Dance Music
Columbia Records (Sony)
New York, New York

How long have you been with Columbia?
DJ: I've been here at Columbia for the last ten years. Prior to that, I worked at Arista Records for ten years who I joined straight out of the University of North Carolina at Chapel Hill.

What are your duties as Senior Director of Dance Music?
DJ: I do two things. One is dance music A&R, which stands for artist and repertoire work and the other is dance music marketing.

So you would have to be a fan of electronic dance music?
DJ: Yes, I go back even before electronic dance music or electronica, back to the early days. I was a fan of people like Simple Minds, Heaven 17, Human League, Gary Numan and Kraftwerk. These were artists that laid the groundwork for the Electronica that's around today.

Did you ever imagine that electronic dance music would become this big?
DJ: It's getting bigger and bigger all the time. Now we are even seeing it embraced by commercial radio stations. We now have a song like "Praise You" by Fatboy Slim making Top 40 radio. That says that this music is now going to the next level.

And there are radio stations in England with DJs playing live, continuous, four-hour mixes?

DJ: There's no doubt about it that England and Europe are really the center of the whole movement. If you look at the artists that are making it in this genre, most of them are coming from the UK or Europe. There's always been such a strong and very exciting scene for this music over there. If you look at people like Underworld or Faithless or Fatboy Slim, they are all coming out of the UK. It's the market that everyone looks to see where the cutting edge is.

How do you find new talent? How do you decide how to market an artist?

DJ: We have a fully staffed A&R department here and Sony (parent company) has a global commitment to find new talent. Not only here but throughout our various territories around the world. For instance, we have a label called Higher Ground in the UK that is very aggressively searching out talent in this genre. They now have Left Field, DJ Rap and Grooverider on their roster.

We try to look at it not just from the standpoint of trying to break a song, but trying to break an artist. We look at what we can do to get club play and radio play and what we can do to market the artist on the retail side. Press has played a very key role in Electronica's growth here in the United States. We see a plethora of publications devoting attention to electronic dance music and that is very exciting. We look to exploit the music in all the different avenues...what can we do from an artist development stand point? What can we do with a video? Maybe the artist has a really good video so we might look for exposure on a local video channel or an MTV ad or a club that is programming videos. Our marketing game plan is based on trying to expose the artist in as many places as possible while letting the artist grow at their own pace while always ensuring that the artist's credibility is never compromised. That's very important. You can't turn Grooverider or DJ Rap into something that they are not. These artists have to live and breathe on their own as artists and it's important to our company to support their musical visions.

*With electronic music developing largely in an underground scene, are
you changing your strategies to connect with the underground?*
DJ: We have to look at the underground because that's where it
all started. What's exciting about this music is that the underground is always changing and so it's always important to keep
abreast of what's going on. But the underground is also
becoming much more overground and becoming bigger and
bigger. We are now seeing these rave events taking place in
concert venues. The other day I saw a flyer for a rave event
taking place on Memorial Day weekend at the South Jersey
convention center. It just shows that it's gone from an underground entity to these big commercial events.

*Do you think that the over-commercialization of the music will be detri-
mental to its development?*
DJ: That's always the danger when something gets popular and a
lot of people start jumping on the bandwagon. But I don't think
that that's anything to worry about—on the contrary, I think it's
a positive—because if big companies get behind it and bring it
to a larger audience that will be a positive thing. Probably the
most exposure that Americans are getting to electronic music
today is through television commercials. A lot of car ads are
using electronica now and that was unheard of four years ago.

How has the proliferation of available technology affected the industry?
DJ: I think that the whole DIY ethic is a good thing. Music has
always been a function of technology and the technology today
is getting better every day. A young person 20 years ago wanted a
guitar or a piano, but a child of the millennium wants two
turntables or studio equipment to make music and that's a big
change. I think that the changes in technology have changed
the definition of what a musician is. Musicians are no longer
defined by a person who strictly plays a conventional musical
instrument. The person who is operating samplers and other
studio equipment is now a legitimate musician.

*What new technologies or factors are contributing to the development of
the electronic music scene?*
DJ: There is no doubt that the Internet is making a big impact
on the development of the electronic music scene. Some of the
most aggressive music fans around are into electronic dance
music and the Internet is a major way that kids are finding out
about the music. They can actually listen to certain broadcasts
through the Internet now and this kind of thing is making
tremendous strides for electronic music. Also, word of mouth is
very important in this scene. Kids talk to each other, they travel

in packs going from rave event to rave event and spread the word that way. And although mainstream radio has yet to embrace dance music, there are a lot of cutting-edge specialty radio shows that have rabid followings that make a big impact in the marketplace. The Solid State show in New York programmed by Liquid Todd is a very important show. In Los Angeles there is Jason Bentley's KROQ Afterhours, in Kansas City there's KLZRs Nocturnal Transmissions by Ray Valasquez. These shows have huge a following that create a lot of word of mouth and have a big impact on sales. Even in places like Champaign, Illinois or York, Pennsylvania they actually have specialty shows that are devoted to this music. We send music directly to these DJs.

What kind of results can you expect from airplay on specialty radio shows?
DJ: It's helping tremendously. For instance we have a group right now, The Low Fidelity All-Stars, who have broken through in a significant manner in the United States. It's through the support of these DJs early on that has really helped pave the way for this groups success today. If you look at the support these DJs have given people like Underworld and Crystal Method you'll see that they have really made a big difference.

In the UK there is a huge proliferation of pirate radio stations. Has this phenomenon spread to the States yet?
DJ: It has, but not anywhere near to the extent that it is in the UK. I think that the radio landscape is different in the UK and creates more of an opportunity to create pirate radio. It's happening in the States too, but on a much, much smaller level. There are some stations in Miami and places like that but they are not a major factor in the growth of electronic music. In the States, college radio plays a bigger role in developing the scene than underground stations. [As we go to press, in a distinct turn-around from previous policy, the FCC is considering authorizing more low-power stations.]

Would you market your releases through pirate radio stations?
DJ: Yes. If there was a DJ who we thought was appropriate we would, and have. There's a DJ called E-Love for instance who spins records for a pirate radio station in Miami and we've sent her stuff.

What differences have you noticed between the American and European markets?

DJ: First, there is a much larger dance culture in Europe and the UK than in the States. Dance music in Europe is the equivalent of hip-hop in the United States. If you go to a newsstand in London, you see Time magazine and five dance publications right next to it. Here in the US it's nowhere near at that level yet, but it's getting bigger and bigger.

In what other countries are you seeing increased interest in electronic dance music?

DJ: The Far East and Japan now have a huge scene for electronic dance music. It's very, very big over there. It's growing all aver the world. A friend of mine recently went to a rave event in Israel and said it was unbelievable. There are now rave events in unthinkable places. Dance music is so universal. It transcends language and so many cultural barriers, which is why it is such a global music. The hot spots right now are England and mainland Europe, followed by Japan and the United States. I should also mention Australia. It's really become a global phenomenon. If you look at DJs like Josh Wink who tour throughout the world to countries like Poland and Greece and all over, we can really see that there is a huge demand for this music.

Do you think there is a danger that electronic musicians and DJs will replace conventional live music?

DJ: They are not going to supplant live performers, there will always be a demand for that. But parallel to that are these DJs who are touring in the same way that rock bands tour and there is a bigger and bigger demand to hear them. Some groups are now taking it to the next level, like Left Field, who started out DJing and are now in an actual live performance situation. The Low Fidelity All Stars have a DJ on stage, but also now tour with a drummer and the whole bit. So, we are seeing more of a hybrid between live performers and DJs.

In a sample-driven genre like this, how can you ensure that everyone gets a credit?

DJ: It's very important from the start to make sure that the sample clearances are taken care of, which is only right because at the end of the day you want to make sure that the music you're utilizing gets some sort of writing credit. If you look at a lot of the big beat music that's coming out now, it's all sample-driven. We always try and make sure we have our samples cleared so we don't have a situation where the record is already out there and all of a sudden there's a sample that's not cleared and you have potential legal problems.

How can you be sure of all the sources of the samples?
DJ: There are now sample clearance companies whose sole job is to clear samples. Also you can go to the artists and ask them what songs they might have sampled. They will usually know their sources.

Will audio tape become obsolete any time soon?
DJ: The tape configuration continues to drop while the CD continues to rise and there is no abating of that trend. If you look at the configuration of single sales for dance music there is no doubt cassette sales are dwindling and the CD is now dominant. Our 12-inch vinyl sales have dropped dramatically as well. DJs are still buying the 12-inch vinyl, but to the consumer there is little to no demand for vinyl. We will continue to release vinyl though because we know there is a demand from the DJ community and we feel that it is important to support that.

Is it cheaper to produce electronic dance music?
DJ: I think so. You can have a home studio in your bedroom and make recordings. That's the beauty about dance music, the investment is comparatively low yet the return is potentially astronomical if you can break through on a global scale. So, on the whole, it's a less expensive music to produce.

What is a white label?
DJ: Prior to the release of the regular promotional copy or the commercial copy of a single, a limited pressing of a 12-inch is made that has little or no copy on the label. These white labels are given to select, key, pacemaker DJs who play them to create an initial buzz. Often it's done on a limited basis and then followed by a regular promotional copy which has the label copy and then, in most cases a regular commercial release. The name comes from the plain white label with nothing on at all.

Would you go back and change the mix on a white label based on feedback from a DJ?
DJ: That could potentially happen but usually what we've come out with has already been "worked" and we feel pretty confident in the mix that we have. What we might do based on that feedback is come up with an additional mix that might broaden the exposure in the clubs.

Electronic musicians are typically unknown to the fans, who are more likely to follow DJs than producers. This must make it harder to market them?

DJ: That is definitely a big problem that the dance music industry is facing and something that we are trying to overcome. There is no doubt about it that when we hear things at the club, it's sometimes hard to identify what record is being heard unless it has an identifiable hook or something. Like I said before, we don't just believe in promoting a single but rather explore all the different avenues to give a face to the music. A lot of the music being played has no real identity to it in terms of who the artist is. A case in point is DJ Rap. We have a single out there right now called Bad Girl and we'll do everything from club promotions with giveaways to have her doing press, radio interviews, promotional tours to try and give a face to the music. We tell people who DJ Rap is and give some identity to her rather than just having the record played in the clubs. Exposure in publications is very important. Dance fans are a very literate and smart group of people. They read magazines a lot and are big Internet users and they find out about who is behind the music.

A lot of DJs are also releasing music with several different labels under various aliases that must confuse things further?

DJ: It's not the ideal situation but it does happen. Someone who has created an identity with some commercial success might still want to do something on the underground so as to not compromise their artistic vision, so they might give themselves a separate identity. It is confusing but I think there are benefits.

Would Columbia Records have a problem with one of their artists releasing underground track under an alias?

DJ: No, not at all. As a matter of fact I think that it can help because as this music gets bigger and bigger I think it's important to never lose sight of the underground roots. Mainstream success comes and goes and there is no guarantee that it will continue at all. When you have a strong underground following, it can continue for a long time and actually sustain careers. We have an artist now called Mousse T with a hit called Horny that has been a huge smash and has now been released in the United States. But as big as he's become, he doesn't want to lose the underground following that has supported him from the beginning, so he also releases underground records and I think that is very smart of him.

What trends do you see in the industry right now?

DJ: I think that we will continue to see more and more kinds of music merge into each other making more hybrids, which will be very exciting. Also we will see all kinds of different artists embraced under the banner of Electronica. If you look at the alternative Essential Beats chart, which I think is a terrific chart that really gives a good fix on what's happening in electronic music, you will see everything from Beastie Boys to Van Helden to Fatboy Slim to the Dub Pistols to Massive Attack. There are distinct differences between these artists but they are all being embraced by the electronic community. I think that's very good for Electronica and very exciting in general. I see this trend continuing to develop into the next decade and I definitely see the music getting bigger too as more and more kids get into it.

Do you see the syncopated, hip-hop based rhythms of drum and bass taking over from the four-four time beats of house and techno?

DJ: Only to a certain degree. If anything, the big beat thing seems to be taking off with people like Fatboy Slim being embraced in a more mainstream way. Hip-hop rhythms are very, very big in the United States right now but the music is constantly changing and reinventing itself all the time and so what we see today could be totally different in a year from now.

What are you working on at the moment?

DJ: Right now we have a lot of very exciting projects we are working on here at Columbia. The Low Fidelity All Stars are getting a lot of critical raves including a major piece in the New York Times. The album is called How to Operate with a Blown Mind and they have just finished a tour across the US. DJ Rap's Bad Girl is zooming up the charts right now. We have a drum and bass DJ called Grooverider who has just released an album called Mysteries of Funk. And we recently released the Left Field album on the Higher Ground label in the UK and on the Columbia label in the United States.

How can electronic musicians contact you?

DJ: The best way is to email me at: **david_jurman@sonymusic.com**

Hook/Bellboy Records
Aberdeen, Scotland.

Fig. #36: Chris Cowie

Chris, what are you working on at the moment?
CC: The current projects that I'm working on is under the pseu-
donym Scan Carriers and it's basically an album worth of
material. In between that I'm still doing the usual dance stuff. I
primarily do dance music, but for the Scan Carriers stuff, I'll be
using guitars and real drummers. I'll end up sampling everything but I'll start out using real people so it's more organic
music like a proper band. That's how I started off years ago. But
I'm not doing the album full time, I'll do a track here and there
in between other stuff for the Hook and Bellboy labels.

Do you make a lot of music under pseudonyms?
CC: Yes, I do. I use Vegas Soul for a tech house kind of thing. X
Cabs is a trance act I do. There are various others I could rattle
off but those are the main three.

*Doesn't it get confusing for the people trying to follow your music to use
so many different names?*
CC: Well, it does. We might get a letter from someone who likes
a Scan Carriers track and they'll be surprised to find out it's me,
but they're generally quite pleased to find that out anyway. I

don't put my name to a lot of stuff I do, I'll just put something like, written and produced by X Cabs. Another example is Stonemaker or Bulkhead, two other names I've used. Nobody likes a smart-ass, you see. They don't like someone who writes too much music and I happen to be able to write a lot of music, which is good for the labels because we can put out a lot of stuff. But I don't think that it's too confusing. I don't think that dance music I make will be around forever. I don't think that in twenty years time I'll be sitting around in the bar singing along to an old X Cabs records. Dance tracks have a relatively short shelf life so rather than me putting out an X Cabs record every week, I'll put stuff out under different names.

How do you organize your time between producing, remixing and any other duties at the labels?
CC: I used to do a lot of Remixes but I've cut back because I have a lot of work to do for the labels. When the labels were launched six years ago, I was the only one doing the music but over the years we've got other artists making music. My time is basically divided into doing music, going home and going out occasionally.

What other artists do you represent?
CC: Well, from America we have Christopher Lawrence, Sandra Collins, a guy called Chris McSpadum from Arizona and Frankie Bones from New York just put out a record on Bellboy. And we've just signed 808 State. We have a roster of about twenty artists in all.

How long have you been in the dance music business?
CC: I started off playing in punk bands and I started playing guitar at twelve. But I've been making electronic music for fifteen years. I started when the first Yamaha sequencer with MIDI came out. Before that you had to use sequencers without MIDI and you had to plug things in. But when MIDI came along, that was it for me. One of my first pieces of equipment was a two-track sequencer from Yamaha.

Can you remember your first impressions of electronic dance music?
CC: When I first got into electronic music, I was still playing in guitar bands. A lot of people will say they heard Kraftwerk first or Jean Michel Jarre or whatever, but they were never really an influence on me. It was listening to people like New Order and Yello and a band called Shriekback in '82 or '83. I was always

drawn to music that sounded electronic. "Can You Feel It" by The Jackson Five from the seventies had a synthesizer kind of sound to it and I would rate that as an electronic type sound.

Do you think that the music being produced in Scotland has a unique sound?

CC: I don't think that there's a characteristic sound. Scotland is quite a small country with only six million people but it has produced a lot of good music of all genres. There are hip-hop labels here and trip-hop and house and techno. So I don't think there is a characteristic sound but Glasgow is known for a deep house sound and most of the clubs there play house music. Here in Aberdeen you can hear anything you want to hear any night of the week in the clubs. Scotland does its own thing but gets its influences from all over the world.

Where do you start when creating a track? Do you have a method?

CC: I could just be sitting in my house listening to something that sounds good and I'll get a wee surge of energy and pop into the studio and start doing something. It's not like you copy it but you just get influenced by something driving down the road. Generally if I go into the studio, I'll start with a bass line or a bass drum but there's no set pattern. It can start with a sample or anything. Some people have a method of working but I think that everyone is creative in their own individual way.

What equipment are you using currently?

CC: I'm a believer in not having too much equipment. There's a lot of people who must buy the latest bit of equipment and I don't do that. I use a Roland S750 Sampler, an Atari 1040 computer, a Mackie SR32, an Ensoniq DP/4 effects unit, a couple of Behringer compressors and a Yamaha GP 8000. I don't have racks of modules and mountains of cables and I'm still using the Atari 1040 with Cubase. When I play live I have a Yamaha O2R which is a much more expensive desk than the one I use in the studio, but it has the recall functions that I need for live performance. I also use an Akai MPC 2000 and an S760 for live gigs.

Does the technology sometimes get in the way of making music?

CC: It can. You can end up spending a lot of time trying out new equipment and forget about making music. When I was younger I went through a period of buying everything and a lot of the time I was let down by it. So now I've trimmed the studio down to the bare necessities. Too much equipment can also slow you down. I know people who can spend two weeks on a track and I can do a track in one day easily. I know my equipment inside out now but if you are constantly buying new equipment you are constantly leaning how to use it. It's very hard to keep up with what's going on and to know what's good and what's not. At the end of the day you never really know if a piece of equipment is any good until you try it out in a real situation.

What are the essential pieces of equipment for an electronic producer?
CC: I would say that the absolute essentials would be a sampler, and if you are just starting out you could pick up an Atari 1040 running Cubase, a mixing desk, an effects unit that can do more than one effect at the same time like a Ensoniq DP/4. And you need a drum machine so that you can free up the sampler because you don't want the sampler to do all the drums. So something like the Novation Drum Station. The last thing would be some kind of sound module, something that you can get strings out of easily. I worked out the cost to buy a set up like this in the States and it came to about $4,000. You don't need to spend $20,000 and get a Mac and a digital hard disk recorder and all that to start.

What new developments do you see on the horizon that will affect the production of electronic dance music?
CC: In the next few years digital desks and mixing consoles like the O2R will get better. People still like to have knobs to play with. Some people will say that mixing consoles will be obsolete because it can all be done with a computer but I don't think that computers are powerful enough to do everything. And even if they could, you'll just be sitting there typing things into the computer and lose a lot of the human element. I think that there will always be people who need "hands on." They want to turn knobs and push buttons. Of course the biggest developments are in computers. Look at Cubase VST and the amount of plug-ins you can get for that. The companies that make effects units must be getting a bit worried because you can buy loads of effects plug-ins quite cheaply for these programs. I've tried some of them and they are very good. But you still can't plug an XLR microphone into the back of a computer yet. All these things will come but I don't think that every producer is going to want to sit there looking at a screen all day. I'm not anti-computers at all but I don't think that people want to do everything with a computer.

Do you see a move away from vinyl in the future?

CC: The quicker DJs stop using vinyl the better. Vinyl is bulky, expensive and noisy. If you are a DJ who makes your own music, you can make your track, burn it on to a CD and go out and play it the same night. From a record company's point of view, it's actually cheaper to make CDs than vinyl. The vinyl thing is a pain in the ass. It just needs a few big-name DJs to start playing CDs and it may catch on. I'm not anti-vinyl but we're into the new millennium and it's kind of outdated. Imagine what the DJ of the future could do with a CD mixer hooked up to a computer. You'd have instant sampling and instant Remixes. The DJ of the future will be a computer whiz kid and also a talented musician.

Some people would argue that vinyl gives a warmer, more human sound?

CC: Yeah, but so what? I've got the Yamaha O2R mixing desk and I don't use it in the studio because it's a cold-sounding desk. If you compare the same track on vinyl and CD, the vinyl has a slightly different sound but it's nothing to worry about. I don't think that people are jumping around in the clubs saying "Yeah, that sounds really warm!" You can barely tell the difference. I think that CDs used to be cold-sounding but they are a lot better today. They sound the same as what comes off the DAT tape. I like the sound of vinyl as well but it sometimes annoys me when we get one of our records and the crackly noises are louder than the music.

Would you agree that more organic sounds are now being used in dance music?

CC: I think that smart producers use organic sounds. But vocals are organic and they've been used in dance music since day one. I don't think there's a conscious trend to go back to organic sounds but smart producers know that to put a little bit of organic feel back into the music will help the track...especially if it's a good track. If you go into a record store you'll probably find nothing organic in 80% of the records. Some times when you hear an acoustic guitar in a break down or whatever you don't know if some guy came in to play the part or not. The samples are so good that you can barely tell the difference now. I can tell the difference but the average club-goer would think that it was a real guitar.

With technology progressing as it is, do you think that computer-based, home recording studios will eventually become a threat to existing record labels?

CC: I think that's quite healthy. The biggest threat to major record companies is the Internet. One guy can basically set up his own label in his house, make music and upload it to anywhere. That's a few years away but it's a scenario that will definitely happen. The technology is not quite fast enough yet. But as for the guy in his basement burning a few CDs, that's not really going to bother the major record labels at all. But the Internet will be a problem for the record stores. If a label like ourselves was able to bypass our distribution and sell direct to the public we'd make a lot more money.

Have you had any offers from major labels to buy you out?

CC: We've had a few people sniffing around but we need a couple of hit records before that can happen. It's not something that we're looking for. If we wanted that we'd move down to London. There are very few independents left and even fewer successful ones. I think that we are successful at what we do. There are a lot of labels that sell maybe a thousand units and we are doing a good bit more than that but I don't think that we are attractive enough for a major to come in and buy us out…maybe in a couple of years.

What are the advantages for a producer to sign with an independent rather than a major label?

CC: It's an advantage to sign with a major if you can get a good advance. If they give you loads of money up front then that's great. But at the end of the day they can sink you. The advances for indie bands are still far more than the advances that dance artists get. Even the majors won't really splash out that much money. The disadvantage is, take a guy that has done a couple of tracks and signs with a major there's a ninety per cent chance that he'll never be heard of again because he won't have had enough time to develop. And when he gets dropped he thinks there something wrong with him and gets writer's block or something. I experienced this with the very first label I signed with. It depends what you are looking for. Are you looking for a lot of money or do you want to get your music out there and survive for a long time? I'm not saying that everybody who signs to a major label will be a disaster, but what tends to happen is the smaller labels get the guys first and then the majors come in and buy their contract. They're better off going to a small label first because these labels are more likely to look after their artists. A small label is a bit more friendly as well.

Do you still think of Hook Records as an underground label?

CC: The label started off pretty much underground and we've built up a very good reputation over the last six years but we still don't have the muscle get a hit record. When dance music first came to the UK a small label could get a hit record. The majors couldn't do it because they didn't understand what was happening. Now the tables have totally turned and a small independent label can't get a hit record. What could happen is we put out a record and a major comes along and wants to license it for twenty grand. That's the only way we could get a hit record. Even if we had a tune that was a definite hit, we don't have the distribution structure or the money behind us to make it happen. But for the moment we are a successful independent and have no aspirations to get a record in the charts. To get a record in the charts you're looking at spending between £50-75,000 and we just don't have that kind of money to gamble. So we would license the track onto a major.

Is it still as exciting as it was when you first started?

CC: Yes, sometimes. I'm in the studio almost every single day so I get a bit tired of it sometimes but the music is still as exciting as ever. I've always been a guy who likes all sorts of music so if I just listen to tracks day in and day out it would do my head in. So I listen to lots of different styles to keep thing fresh.

What is it that makes this music so exciting?

CC: People like to dance and jump about. Before dance music came along, people would dance to bands like Duran Duran and get up and dance to one or two songs and sit down again. When dance music came along, people got up and danced all night. I think that on some kind of tribal level, people just like to dance. You can basically put on a drum machine in a nightclub and people will dance to that all night. My father likes to ask me when this dance music thing is going to stop, but it's not going to stop because it is the new rock and roll. I don't know where it will be in ten years but I'm 99% certain that people will still want to dance.

Does it bother you that dance music fans tend to follow the DJs playing the records rather than the musicians who make the music?

CC: I could be hated for this comment, but sometimes I get annoyed by DJs when they do interviews and they say "my music." It's not their music. They may be the new pop stars but I think that a lot of them are overrated. At the end of the day they are just putting two records together and playing someone else's music. It's not like a bee in my bonnet or anything but there have been some interviews with big-name DJs that have really annoyed me. If all these small labels stopped putting out these records they wouldn't have any of this music and be making the money they're making. I hear fans saying that a certain DJ is really brilliant but they are only brilliant because they're playing some guy's records that are brilliant. Some big-name DJs are getting paid, say twenty grand, to do a mix CD. So he mixes up his twenty favorite records and that twenty grand comes off the royalties of the record. If it sells fifty thousand units, we'll be lucky to see a grand. It's not really fair that the DJ gets more money than the musician. But DJs do bring in money for the small labels when they use their tracks and provide a bit of exposure. But it would be nice if some of these guys would sometimes mention a few of the labels and put in a good word here and there.

The Internet

MP3 PLAYERS

You will need to download and install an MP3 player before you can play MP3s on your computer. To download an MP3 player, simply go to one of these sites and follow the simple downloading instructions. Often using a familiar looking tape transport or a jukebox look, MP3 players are a simple-to-use interface that connect the user to a far-reaching and sophisticated technology.

Fig. #37: WinAmp MP3 player, user interface

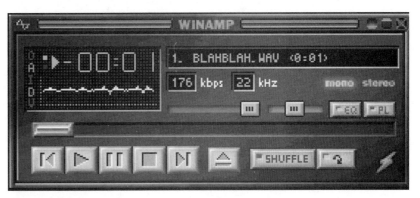

<u>List of Sites:</u>
http://www.mp3yes.com/mp3players.html
http://mp3software.simplenet.com/main.html

Sonique—Sonique features support for all the latest audio formats, a killer user interface, customizable skins and visuals, and built-in access to music resources on the Web.

Napster—A global on-line community discussing and sharing music sites from around the world.

PCDJ Phat (32-bit)-(1.5 MB) The ultimate PC entertainment center. Mix MP3 files, play CDs, rip CDs, play videos, listen to Internet radio, and much more.

Winamp (32-bit)-(476 KB) The best MP3 player for layer 3 MPEG files.

Music Match—Requirements: Windows 95/98/NT, 16 MB RAM (32 MB for NT4), 30 MB available disk space. Pentium 166MHZ or greater and 32 MB of RAM recommended.

Microsoft Media Player (32-bit)-(3.0 MB) Newest version from Microsoft that now handles MP3 files.

K-Jofol (433 KB) Get plenty of extra features with this MP3 player.

WPlay (584 KB) Top rated MP3 player.

DJ2000 (1.3 MB) Good MP3 player.

MP3 SITES

In addition to the barrage of illegal activity, there are hundreds of legal MP3 websites that offer every type of music imaginable. Bypassing the A&R (artists and repertoire) route of the traditional record business, these sites offer the ability for anyone to release their music to a worldwide audience. Instead of relying only on your local music scene to promote your music, an MP3 site allows your work to be heard instantly in almost any corner of the earth. That's very exciting, considering the challenges of traditional promotion.

MP3, with is its high compression/high-quality capabilities, offers a very effective alternative to the cost of producing your own CD or vinyl. MP3 promises to level the music industry playing field by giving artists and labels the freedom to market and distribute their material in any way they please.

Musicians and producers now have access to the largest audience available in any one medium. This is good news for unsigned artists, as it provides a cost-effective method of promotion and distribution. Some would argue that currently, artists are in a position similar to busking on the street corner and placing a "tip hat" on the sidewalk for contributions; with so much out there, it's hard to get noticed. But as with any endeavor, the cream will rise to the top. In the case of the Internet, the process is propelled by word of mouth, which moves around the world literally at the speed of light.

Loss of sales and copyright royalties has become a major concern to many established artists and labels. Recently, Alanis Morrisette became one of the first, most established artists, to release her latest album as a free MP3 file. She felt that offering her work in this way would put her more in touch with her audience and gambled that it would not affect her CD sales too drastically. Some artists have come to believe that MP3 can actually serve to promote their album sales. But the reality of the record business is that artists make far more from touring, merchandising, and corporate tie-ins than they make from selling CDs. Giving the music away to gain greater income from other sources doesn't look like such a bad idea.

You can find just about anything you're looking for on the well-established forums such as MP3.com and Amazon.com, but don't hesitate to surf the web to find more obscure and specialized sites. So, go online and say "I want my MP3!"

COPYRIGHT PROTECTION

Worried about copyright? Copyright protection is a major concern and many artists choose to avoid the Internet for this reason. Luckily, there are more and more new companies that are addressing piracy issues by developing specialized websites that offer protected streaming audio files and MP3 files which can be purchased with a credit card and downloaded in seconds. Major record labels are beginning to use these services as a way of promoting a new release. Previews are often featured that give the listener a free abbreviated version of the recording. Oddly enough, the "single release" is making a comeback and you can purchase one cut for a very nominal price. Here are some of the "legit" online options.

Liquid Audio

Liquid Audio is a leading provider of services and software that enable musicians, record labels and music retailers to deliver professional-quality music digitally via the Internet. Formed by music industry veterans and professional recording engineers, Liquid Audio is spearheading the convergence of music and technology to establish the Internet as a new medium for music distribution. The company's products and services are based on an open architecture that supports many leading digital music formats, including Dolby AC3, AAC, and MP3. This open architecture will also enable Liquid System products to be compliant with the goals of the Record Industry Association of America's

Secure Digital Music Initiative (SDMI), a sort of copy protection for online music.

Liquid Audio gives fans convenient access to downloadable music at the click of a mouse. Using the free Liquid Player, fans can sample music from the Liquid Music Network, check out liner notes, album art, and download promotional or for-sale singles right to a PC. Digital delivery of downloadable music provides fans with instant musical gratification; also, it's easy to take the music on the road by burning custom CDs using a compatible recordable CD drive, or with one of the new portable MP3 players. The Liquid Audio Network comprises hundreds of affiliate websites that offer every type of content imaginable.

SPOTLIGHT ON VISIOSONIC PCDJ PHAT™

Fig. #38: New comer Visiosonic, offers innovative software that enables MP3 files to be mixed on a PC.

VisioSonic- PCDJ PHAT™

A newcomer to the world of MP3, *VisioSonic* has recently gained attention for its innovative software that enables PC users to mix MP3 files "live" on screen. Also offering specialized computers with dual sound cards and a hard drive that will hold up to 10,000 songs, VisioSonic is clearly focused on MP3 as the wave of the future, as explained in the following article by Christopher Jones.

Digital DJs Phatten Up
Article By Christopher Jones

After Nullsoft's Winamp player turned MP3 music into a mainstream phenomenon, a Florida-based software company is trying to turn novice PC users into digital DJs. VisioSonic is offering free downloads of its PCDJ Phat software, which has standard features such as MP3 ripping, play lists and MP3 search tools.

On top of it all, PCDJ Phat includes two players so two music files can play simultaneously with settings to control the interplay, speed, fade and other elements of the playback.

On top of its audio features, PCDJ Phat also has a video window, and lets users play Microsoft's Windows media videos and music simultaneously. It also includes a mini-browser for music searches and surfing.

While it is not the first DJ software to hit the Net, PCDJ Phat is the first free software that bundles everything needed for entry-level users to download, organize, and fiddle with multimedia files on a PC.

Jorgen Hedberg, who developed the software, used to be a DJ and programmer in Sweden and developed the software using his skills in both arenas.

"I used to Remix at home on tape and CD-R, but I wanted to do these things right at the club, then and there. I wanted to do more than just play music, I wanted to perform and create a unique experience for the crowd."

Hedberg said that he originally had the idea for digital DJ software in the late 1980s, but the technology of the time wouldn't allow it. When he saw the MP3 movement beginning several years ago, though, he began to create a set of digital DJ tools.

"As a DJ, I am used to the hardware implementations they have on dual CD players and samplers. So I wanted to emulate the hardware as much as possible and work in a way that I was used to."

Sean Engeldinger, a longtime club DJ who uses VisioSonic's high-end DJ software at gigs, said he also uses the program as a training tool for novice DJs working in small towns.

"All these clubs in places like rural Iowa – the DJs have no training when it comes to beat mixing and how to mix music, and the philosophy of it," he said. "Instead of trying to find a song where you're flipping through a record case or a CD rack, you can just hit 'find' and up it pops. It's very slick."

Marc Simony, a spokesman for SS7X7.com, said he doesn't expect serious DJs to jump on the MP3 bandwagon, but does see a new generation of novice DJs developing.

"I can't say I know of any DJs that use it [PC mixing software]. First of all, they are very comfortable with vinyl, and it's an extension of their arms and hands and it's tough to re-learn that craft in a digital environment...vinyl still rules the day for serious DJs that do more than just segue from one record to the other.

"But how many serious DJs are there compared to bedroom DJs? Nobody will ever hear the terrible fruits of my labor, but it's fun," he added.

Virtual Turntables was one of the first MP3 DJ programs to hit the Net and has already spawned some laptop DJs. There are also more sophisticated DJ tools on the market, like BPM Studio—but the cheapest version of the software costs US$99 and requires 128MB of RAM.

VisioSonic also has plans to drive music fans to its site by hosting and broadcasting events over the Net. Recently, the company began broadcasting 24/7 with 8 channels of Net radio in Microsoft's streaming media format.

SHAREWARE

Perhaps one of the most exciting aspects of music on the Internet is the amazing array of shareware programs that are available for downloading. A great way to sample almost any program imaginable, shareware usually offers a free demo version of an actual program that provides a real feel for the software before you purchase. Sites such as Hit Squad **http://www.hitsquad.com/smm** offer a wide variety of programs that are organized by category and are bound to interest almost anyone. Log on and check out some of the titles for yourself. It's easy and fun.

With the advent of streaming audio, the world of dance-oriented radio has found its way into thousands of homes around the globe. With a computer and a set of speakers, anyone can enjoy music of their choice any time of the day or night. Particularly valid in North America, where there is no established modern dance radio format, Internet radio stations have become an essential link to the global dance scene. All you need to tune in is a copy of the RealAudio™ player that can be downloaded from RealNetworks at **http://www.real.com**. Whether you live in New York City or Minot, North Dakota, you can be in touch with the very latest music trends by checking out any one of the many new Internet radio stations. You will find that many stations are open to giving your music a play and some even will even welcome you as a guest on their live program.

The Beta Lounge Internet radio station- (http://www.betalounge.com)

The Beta Lounge is a new music showcase transmitted live over the Internet every Thursday from 7 p.m. to 11 p.m. PDT from the San Francisco studios of the Network Syndicate. Featuring streaming audio and video presentations, The Beta Lounge is one the originators of Internet radio programming. All shows are archived immediately following the live event, and are available on the site throughout the week.

The Beta Lounge uses the Real Networks streaming media system to deliver real-time audio and video to its listeners. In order to listen to the Lounge, you'll need to get the latest (non-beta) RealMedia Player. With live presentations, you can also try Graham Technology Solutions' "no-helper, no-plug-in" Java audio stream. You'll find both audio streams through the links on their 'Live' page.

Co-founder of the Beta Lounge Internet Radio Station

The Beta Lounge could almost be the granddaddy of Underground Internet Radio. Where and how did it get started?

ZV: The Beta Lounge began as a Sunday afternoon party three years ago above a chicken joint in San Francisco. We were doing web casting and had ISDN, and put it on the net because we could...over time there were more people listening live than there were at the party...

If you log on to the Beta Lounge, you can select live audio and video. How does this work?

ZV: You click the headphones and hear the latest show in excellent quality Real Audio. You'll only get video when we're live. The shows are 4-5 hours and we've had some great parties.

It seems that you offer a wide variety of electronic music styles. Is there a set format? How do you decide what the content will be?

ZV: For the most part the Beta Lounge has consistently been about music of the underground: music being played in clubs and ignored, or at least off the radar screen of the majors. The three main people that do the booking are Ian Raikow, Brian Benitez, and David Goldberg - each of them has slightly different tastes and directions in music and that is reflected in the archive. Another major influence is who happens to be coming through San Francisco, since this is where we are based.

Any live broadcast is challenging. You must have some great stories about certain shows. Can you give us an example?

ZV: MC dynamite and Roni Size live for a packed house - MC dynamite freestyling on what and who he saw around the studio. Power failure and ensuing emergency generator delivery for the Dego show, Shizou of Harcore on the hand-held sampler and mic punk style. Soundlab blowing out the house, the marathon live Systemwide show with 8 live performers.

Are you closely connected with the scene in San Francisco or is it more Global?

ZV: Our supporters and audience are definitely global. Physically we operate out of San Francisco but have part of our crew based in Hamburg, Germany. We definitely consider ourselves part of an international scene of emerging music and culture.

Do you track your listeners and if so who and where are they?
ZV: We don't do extensive tracking- no cookies or clickstream analysis - but of the 80,000 times the show gets listened to a month, and the regular mail we get from our audience, they are mostly in the US and Europe,- with a large percentage coming from Germany. Most of them have constant access to the net at high bandwidth and listen to a lot of music.

It seems that sites like yours are crucial to dance culture in North America, as there are no commercial stations that play Electronica. Do you think that you and other stations provide this link?
ZV: Yes, net radio and the club scene are really the only outlets for this music in the United States.

The UK and much of Europe have commercial dance radio stations. Do you think that this will catch on in North America?
ZV: Not until the majors embrace it, but then it will happen immediately.

How many people does it take to produce your live show?
ZV: At least three. One to DJ, one on the mic, and one to press go. But it's usually a crew of 5, at least 3 DJs, and an audience of 10-50.

How do DJs and remixers audition to be on Beta Lounge?
ZV: It depends who they are. Telephone, email, mp3.

What is the Network Syndicate?
ZV: A crew of good friends that have made the beta lounge happen together since it started.

How many stations like yours do you think are operating in the US?
ZV: I really don't know. Dozens? Hundreds worldwide?

How is the station funded?
ZV: We make some advertising revenue and run a little store, and otherwise self-fund it.

What is your overall philosophy with Beta Lounge?
ZV: Everyone here probably has their own philosophy. Mine is build it yourself. If anything its about being a global forum for electronic music culture and doing something useful and real with the web.

SmashTV is also one of your affiliates. What is this about?
ZV: SmashTV is a broadband development studio that operates a webcast facility in San Francisco. We do creative and technical development for online education and entertainment content.

How can we reach the Beta Lounge?
ZV: You can get us all at **info@betalounge.com**

If you are a DJ, producer, musician, or multimedia artist, and are interested in appearing at the Beta Lounge, send a sample of your material to:

Beta Lounge c/o
Network Syndicate
1072 Illinois St.
San Francisco, CA 94107
http://www.betalounge.com
Send email to **info@betalounge.com.**

Artist Interviews

AN INTERVIEW WITH JOHN DIGWEED

Fig, # 39: John Digweed

John Digweed is a craftsman and an artist whose passion for playing music emerged at the tender age of 15. In the ensuing years he has become one of the most respected and revered figures of the international dance scene and was recently voted #7 in the prestigious DJ Magazine list of Top 100 DJs.

Since founding Bedrock Records ten years ago in Hastings, England, Digweed has sold hundreds of thousands of mix CDs worldwide and is one of the most sought after DJs and remixers in dance music today. Famous for his extended sets and his residency at New York's Twilo Club with long-time partner Sasha, Digweed's star continues to rise. Check out Bedrock's website at **www.bedrock.org.uk**.

How is your schedule these days?
JD: It not so much that I'm doing loads of gigs, but I'm doing so much traveling and I'm trying to do some Remix work as well. I've literally been getting off the plane, having a quick sleep, driving for two hours up to the studio, coming back and doing other work, like organizing club nights.

Do you have a tour manager to make sure that you are making connections along the way?
JD: No, but I have management that sorts things out for me. I like to drive myself when I can.

Do you have many problems with parties being canceled?
JD: No, not really. A lot of the parties I play are in clubs.

Do you ever miss the old days of illegal underground warehouse parties?
JD: No, but I think that there was a definite element of excitement when we were running around in farmer's fields to a marquis tent with the decks on the back of a lorry, not knowing if it was going to be shut down, and watching the sun come up in the morning. There was a lot of fun about those days. I've been privileged to have witnessed both sides of it. I enjoy playing in clubs like Twilo but I like the fact that I played at those early parties as well. That's where I cut my teeth.

Did you start off on the dance floor?
JD: No. I've always been behind the decks. I've got two left feet so I've never been much of a dancer.

When and where did you first hear electronic dance music?
JD: I've always been into music from the word go. I was really into New Order and the alternative stuff like Bauhaus, but at the same time I was also into soul and funk and then later electro and hip-hop. As new stuff came along I was reading magazines and always trying to stay on top of things. I can remember when all the early DJ International stuff and the Chicago tracks started coming to the UK. That's when I started thinking that things were really stepping up a peg or two. The kick drums and everything were just so in-your-face and that's when house music really grabbed hold of me.

Did you get a sense back then that we were on the verge of a musical revolution?

JD: Not really. When I first started DJing, I was doing most of the gigs for nothing, or just enough money to buy a few more records. I did it for the love of it. There was no traveling the world and being written about in magazines. It was very much a passion for music and having a way to express it. For me, it was always about the buzz of creating a party atmosphere and being able to play and making people enjoy themselves.

Is it still as exciting as it was?

JD: Totally. Even more so now. There is a whole new generation coming to hear the music now. They have been waiting in the wings because they haven't been old enough to get into the clubs and they've heard about the DJs through their brothers and sisters and magazines and they're keen as mustard to get stuck in. People that come to clubs now are a lot more aware of the scene than they were years ago. I think it's good. It's a healthy thing.

Have you noticed a difference between American audiences and English audiences?

JD: Well, I've been coming to America for five years now and the music we play isn't on the radio like it is in England where you have Pete Tong and Rampling and all that lot playing to the whole nation. In America it's smaller and more underground but the kids that do know their stuff really know the music and are really into it. They come up after I play and they know half my set and what tracks I've played. There's such a fresh energy in the States. In England a lot of the people take the music for granted. I feel that I have the best of both worlds because I play amazing parties in both England and America.

What about the scene in other countries, like South Africa?

JD: The first time Sasha and I went down there, we played at a party with sixteen thousand people and last December I played a party with eight thousand people in a railway building. It was incredible, the place just went mad and they are really into it.

What other countries have you played in recently?

JD: I played in Costa Rico and Uruguay. I was scheduled to play Brazil recently but I had bronchitis so I had to cancel. I'll be going to Brazil again later this year. I did Moscow this year and that was great. It's a bit weird because you don't know who's in charge and you have to watch out who you bump into. It was very interesting because for the first fifteen minutes of the set they were just kind of standing there watching and checking out what I was doing and I was thinking, Oh no, I'm not sure they are getting it. Then after about twenty minutes the place started going mad. It wasn't like England where you put your first record on and everyone goes mad. It was a little bit nervy to start with but that's okay because it keeps you on your toes.

Did you see some of the same dance fashions in Russia that we have in North America?

JD: It was a very smart set. There's a very small percentage of people in Russia who have all the money and everyone else is completely broke. Obviously the parties attract the people with money. There were some very trendy people but more clubby than ravey.

Are there any interesting Russian electronic musicians or DJs?

JD: They had a live PA at the party I played with a guy who was the No. 1 Russian techno artist. He was up there on a keyboard going bonkers and was very interesting. It's a problem getting equipment out there and at the moment. It's quite limited in terms of what equipment they can get.

Are you mostly playing acetates or slates these days?

JD: Not really, but obviously I get a lot of producers who give me DATs and acetates, but I don't just play acetates because it's an acetate. The reason I play a record is because I think that it's good. I get a lot of up-front stuff sent to me and I think that people do expect to hear a lot of new music when I play. I try and mix up stuff that people might know with stuff that they don't know and try for a happy mix. Sometimes it might be a fifty-fifty mix but sometime I might just be playing imports or European stuff. There's no real ratio because it changes week by week.

Do record companies give you acetates in the hope of feed back on which to plan Remixes?

JD: Most of the time the Remix is already done. They might have got six mixes done and they will send out the acetates. But they might just put one twelve inch out with two mixes on and rely on the feedback from DJs to decide which mixes to use. It's quite a privileged position to be in.

Some other DJs are saying that this will be the year of trance. Do you agree?

JD: It's very popular in America now and looking at the winter music conference this year in Miami there was a big progressive sound there with Paul van Dyk, Paul Oakenfold, Sasha, and myself all doing big nights. It was bigger this year than any year since the Miami conference started and judging by the reaction it seemed very popular.

We went from house to progressive house and from techno to trance and now we have progressive trance. Is there really a difference?

JD: I'm not really into all these pigeonholes. I play records because I like them not because of what genre they are. I think that these categories are just stuff that journalists invent. I play elements from many different styles and I don't worry about what side of the fence it's on.

Do you ever Remix break beat records?

JD: Yes, last year, I did a Remix of a band called Terminal Head and the tracks called Weekend Warriors. It will be out soon on Push Recordings.

What are the qualities in Electronic dance music that affect people so deeply?

JD: I think that there is a lot of emotion in the tracks and it brings a lot of people together. A lot of friendships have been made out of this music and people have shared great nights together. People have a lot of fond memories from going out and listening to the music. It's very powerful. Electronic music is playing a massive part in a lot of the films being made today as well. You'll be watching a scene in a film and an Underworld track will come on and send shivers up your spine.

How do you see electronic music developing in the future?

JD: I have no idea. It is changing at such a rapid rate that it would be really hard to predict. But I think it will just get bigger. In the last five or six years I've seen it become a huge worldwide scene. I play in countries all over the world and get pretty much the same reaction everywhere I go. I think that in the future we will see more and more people making electronic music in pockets all over the world, taking elements from different cultures and just keep on growing. The music is truly international. I can be playing in Russia and not speak a word of the language, but there are smiles on their faces and they're enjoying the music as much as anywhere I go.

Who are the most promising and talented electronic musicians today?
JD: There are some guys from Manchester called Fluid that have been around for a while but are putting out some really good tracks. A guy called Breeder from Cambridge is doing some very cool stuff. I get a lot of white labels from the States but half the time I don't know who the artists are, but there is a lot of good music coming out of America like the Deep Sky Boys, Sandra Collins, The Fade, BT, and Taylor. I think that there will be a lot more good music coming out of America in the near future.

Do you pre-plan your sets or just go with the flow?
JD: Just go with the flow. I think it's a mistake to try and plan a set because you don't know what the nights going to be like. You could plan a set that's totally wrong for the crowd.

Do you still get nervous before playing to big crowds?
JD: I'm pretty nervous before I do any gig, whether it's hundred people or ten thousand. But I think that it's good to have some nerves because it shows that you care about what you are doing. Once you get in there and play a couple of records, you can start to relax and get into your stride.

How did you come to team up with Sasha?
JD: Because we have really similar tastes in music and a similar approach to DJing. Although we DJ differently we complement each other and both understand how a whole night works, how it should be built up, where to put the mood changes etc. We are very like-minded, but if you gave us both ten records we would both mix them differently.

As a DJ, what are your responsibilities to an audience?
JD: To give them a good time, but also to educate them. There's a lot of new music out there and for me it's far more rewarding to play a track that no ones heard before and programming it at the right time so the place goes absolutely mad rather than playing an obvious record that you know will get a big reaction. It's easy to put on a big record and get a big reaction.

Do you think there is a trend towards DJs wanting to do more to influence the music they are playing by using more equipment on stage?
JD: Yes, definitely. I've had the Numark 1975 mixer for ten years now and it has a little sampler and effects unit. It's been a great little tool but when you start getting things like The Filter Factory from Electrix where you can really buck up the sounds, that will take it to the next level.

How do you approach a Remix and what equipment do you use?

JD: The last thing we did was with Danny Tenaglia's "Turn Me On." We wanted to do something that complemented the track but give it a tougher British sound with a New York influence. So we filtered the vocals up in the Akai 3000 and used a Juno 106 and a sampler.

What software are you using?

JD: I use Notator on an Atari. Nick Muir, who I work with, knows the Atari inside out and he does all the programming.

I thought that Atari was obsolete?

JD: (Laughs) Yes, they are. It's not very fast, but Nick's very fast. William Orbit did most of his mixes on Atari. It's all down to knowing your equipment. You can have the fastest computer in the world but it's no good unless you know how to use it. When I did the Northern Exposure records with Sasha we used Pro Tools for edits and filtering but when we do Remixes we use the Atari.

How long does it take you to do a Remix and do you have a set method of working?

JD: Maybe a day or two pre-production and then two days to mix it down. The method varies each time. If it's a song then we'll try and work stuff around the song. If it's an instrumental we'll work on rhythms and moods.

What are the essential pieces of equipment for a beginning producer?

JD: A sampler, a fairly decent keyboard and a computer. But you could probably do as well starting out with an Akai MPC 3000 which is a drum machine, sequencer and sampler in one. You can do amazing stuff on that.

What are you working on at the moment?

JD: I'm doing a Remix for Fire Island and there's a couple of tracks that we've started work on about eight months ago. But due to my schedule, I haven't had a chance to finish them.

Do you have a studio in your house?

JD: No, I work at a friend's place. He has a set up in a loft and we do all the pre-production work there, then we go into a big studio to do the final mix down. The studio is in London so it's a two hour drive there and two hours back.

Geographically, where are the new hot spots for electronic dance music?
JD: I think that America is really hot at the moment. Australia is always good, and Ibiza in the summer is amazing.

Where do you see yourself in five years time?
JD: Hopefully still championing the sound and continuing to play a part in something that I really enjoy and feel passionate about.

INTERVIEW WITH DAVE RALPH

Fig. #40: Dave Ralph

Dave Ralph, known for his energetic and uplifting sets, has been DJing and rocking dance floors for over two decades. A native of Manchester, England, he recently embarked on an intensive North American tour with Paul Oakenfold. After a long distance game of cell phone tag, we finally caught up with him in Panama City.

Where are you now?
DR: Panama City. We did a party last night, then we're doing Tallahassee tonight, New York tomorrow night, then we're off to Toronto and then Cuba.

When and where did you first hear house music?
DR: The first time I heard house music was on a radio station called Q103 in Manchester, played by a guy called Stu Allen. The first track I heard was Mr. Finger's Washing Machine. This was very early track stuff around '86 or '87. They used to scratch and

cut things up all over it. I loved it immediately, thought it was amazing and had to go all the way to London to about four shops to find the records. There was an old woman who must have been around seventy who worked at Groove Records who totally understood house music. She had Traxx records which were pressed on second hand vinyl. They used to take old K-Tel LPs and re-press right on top of them. They always sounded bloody terrible, but you had the music.

What are the current trends in electronic music and where is it going?
DR: Right now, trance has become incredibly popular in the UK, all over Europe and America and becoming more and more popular by the day. A lot of DJs are really getting into that sound and for me it's a way forward. I don't play break-beat, but I know that people like the Chemical Brothers are incredibly popular. As for where the music is going to go next, I think that things just keep developing and moving on, new sounds keep coming in and people keep pushing the boundaries.

What are the qualities that make electronic dance music so popular with so many people?
DR: I think it's the melody and emotion in it. If you listen to trance music you'll hear a lot of emotion and feeling in it. If you are on a dance floor with six or seven hundred other people and you hear those lush strings and beautiful melodies it has a euphoric effect and there's nothing wrong with a bit of euphoria. That's what it does for me. These tracks really take you somewhere and a good DJ puts these elements together and creates a journey. The reception we are getting to this music in America is incredible, it's very encouraging.

Do you see DJs using more equipment on stage in the future, like the Chemical Brothers or Prodigy?
DR: I don't see why they shouldn't. It's not the most difficult job in the world to put two records together and if you can make that sound more interesting by adding more technology then I'm all for it. As long as it's not overdone. I find that some people with those Pioneer mixers just go on and on and on, flanging and phasing or whatever. Sometimes less is more. I think that ease of use is important and whether you can under-stand it quickly and put it into effect.

What basic equipment would a mid-range producer need today to start making tracks?

DR: It's all down to how much money you have. There are so many innovative ideas out there now but they cost a lot of money. I think that the two pieces of essential equipment would be a mixing desk and a computer that's fast enough to do what you want it to do. Then you can find software these days that will do anything. If some one gave me 10,000 pounds ($24,000), which is not a lot of money to spend on a small studio, I would spend the majority on a mixing desk, a computer with software and a key board of some sort.

Do you plan your sets? Do you have a method or system?

DR: I look at the crowd. At the end of the day, those kids are paying my wages and I have a responsibility to entertain them. I'm not into the idea of putting your head down and concentrating on what you're doing and ignoring the crowd. I will walk into a room and look at the people and listen to the other DJs, and based on that, I will choose records that will pull people into my sound. It might take me twenty minutes to get them there. If they're not dancing you have to move on. I don't think that a lot of DJs do that.

What are the lessons we can learn from rave culture or dance music culture?

DR: I think that it has brought people together. I've been DJing for twenty-one years and looking back to when I first started, people were dancing in clubs but there was never that feeling of oneness. After the rave scene happened people got into the whole vibe of it and broke down a lot of barriers. People were able to smile at each other or shake hands or give each other a hug. It has definitely brought people closer. The people who go to event today are far more relaxed and chilled-out than the people who used to go to night clubs fifteen years ago and dance to Donna Summer or whatever. If you walk into a rave club now it's a happy vibe and that's really nice to see.

Fig. # 41: Paul Oakenfold

Paul Oakenfold is a true giant in the world of electronic dance music. From his early career as a hip-hop promoter and agent for the likes of The Beastie Boys and Run DMC, he has always been on the cutting edge of new music. Paul was there at the very beginning in Ibiza where itinerant Brits first began staging all-night electronic dance parties and was one of the first people to bring this new cultural phenomenon back to England.

In 1985 he opened the first rave club in the UK called The Fun House and later The Project Club and The Future, all of which introduced emerging electronic dance forms to English music fans eager for something new and exciting. This, in turn, led to the birth of the acid house movement in the UK and eventually to the global rave movement. The rest, as they say, is musical history.

Almost two decades later, Paul Oakenfold continues to break new ground as a producer, re-mixer and DJ. Three times he has been voted DJ of The Year and this year was voted World's No.1 DJ by the readers of DJ Magazine. As well as being one of the most sought after DJs in the world, Paul still find time to runs his UK based record label, Perfecto. Along with Frankie Knukles and David Morales, Oakenfold is also one of the world's busiest re-mixers, fending off a half dozen remix offers a week! Over the past few years he has re-mixed everyone from the Rolling Stones to Snoop Dogg to the Smashing Pumpkins and U2.

Do you find that North American audiences are different than UK audiences?
PO: No, not that much different. They seem to be very open-minded and going with it, so it's great. But I think it's pointless for me to come over here and play American music. I have to give them something new, so that's what I'm doing.

When and where did you first hear house?
PO: Probably at the Paradise Garage in New York in '84. Larry Levan was there at the time and the tracks were coming out of Chicago and Detroit.

What was the scene like in Ibiza in 1985?
PO: There wasn't much going on in Ibiza then. It was all underground and people were just starting to get into it.

And you brought that underground scene back to the UK?
PO: Yeah, I was running a club which closed at 2 a.m. and then we started up an illegal after-hours club. We'd kick everyone out at two, open the back door and carry on until six and that's how we started the underground scene. That was in '87.

The terms progressive and trance seem to be almost interchangeable these days. What's the difference between progressive house and trance?
PO: Trance is faster and more melodic and progressive has more drops in it. But it's definitely getting closer. Trance is becoming really big now everywhere.

What are the qualities in this music that affect people so deeply?
PO: The energy, the melody. It's uplifting and spiritual. There's a lot of soul in it and it really is about the feeling. It's similar to soul music in that you listen to it from an emotional standpoint.

Some people view the DJ as a kind of Shaman or spiritual guide who leads the listeners from one level of consciousness to another. Do you agree?
PO: Absolutely. That's what I mean to do is take you on a spiritual journey.

What are the responsibilities that come with being in such a position of power?

PO: It's no different than a lead singer in a band. You're there to entertain and educate and there's a fine line between the two. People pay money to come and see you so they expect you to deliver and, as a professional, I take that very seriously and do my best. Not everyone is going to like everything you do but at least you can take them somewhere they've never been before. You just have to be open-minded and go with it and I find that people in America and Canada are doing just that.

How do you decide which records to play when?

PO: The two most important records of the night are the first and the last. Then there's getting from one point to the other and building an arrangement and structure. A minor key will make you feel solemn and a major key will make you feel happy. It's what you fill in between and where you go with it. I need to find my rhythm in the journey and sometimes it comes right away and sometimes it takes time to get the crowd to where you want them to be. I can usually get there in a half-hour and then take it to where I want to go depending on how I feel at the time. A three-hour mix is really one record with a start, a middle, and an outro. I approach a three hour set the same way I would approach mixing a record.

How was the reception in Vancouver, Canada?

PO: That was my first time in Vancouver and they sold out. It was a good party and it was good to see that people came out, had a great time and were open-minded. And a lot of the records I played were on acetate so it's not like they'd heard the music before. People were really going with it. I found that Canadians were more up for it than the Americans. I think Canadians are more ahead of the game and more aware and educated about the music.

Do you see a trend towards DJs using more equipment on stage?

PO: That's been developing for a long time. I've used live guitarists and live percussion. I've used vocalists and MCs and programmed drum machines. But it's a fine line because you can program all your own rhythms and nobody really knows you're mixing them in.

How do you plan your time between producing, DJing, and re-mixing?
PO: I just do things when I feel like it. I get offered about five to seven mixes a week and I do them if I want to do them. I produced Happy Monday's single just before I went on tour and I have no plans to get back in the studio when I get home, but if something comes along that I like, then I'll do it. It's really that simple.

Is dance culture still growing?
PO: In the UK and Europe, youth culture *is* dance culture now. You've got twenty-four hour dance radio and the biggest rock bands in the world who all want dance re-mixes. The majority of the pop charts are dance music. One of the biggest music publications recently reported that turntables are now out selling guitars three to one. So there's a big shift. Young people want to buy turntables and be DJs today. Dance music is more accessible now, you can make a dance record in your bedroom and in the UK a dance record can sell two million copies.

AN INTERVIEW WITH JAMES LUMB OF ELECTRIC SKYCHURCH

Fig. #42: James Lumb

Los Angeles veteran Electronica producer James Lumb has been churning out tracks as "Electric Skychurch" since 1989.

James began as a bass player for the underground psychedelic funk band the Groove Trolls way back in 1987 and in 1989, armed with a drum machine and a 4-track, he started writing acid house tracks. At the time, Los Angeles' rave scene was exploding so James abandoned the bass and picked up a sampler. In the spring of 1992, working alone, he released the first "Electric Skychurch" single on cassette.

In the spring of 1993, David Delaski joined the band. Shortly thereafter, James and a small group of friends decided to have a party in the desert. That party, the "Full Moon Gathering," also happened to be the first "Electric Skychurch" live show. One party led to another and pretty soon they evolved into the full-blown "Moontribe" movement.

In 1988, they hit the road with DJ John Kelley and played eighty shows around the world. Armed with a full band—drummer Alex Spurkel and singer Roxanne Morganstern—as well as a light show and DJ entourage they played to over a quarter-million people proving to be one of America's few big electronic acts.

Original recordings like Creation, Deus, Knowonenes, and the popular Together CD have earned James Lumb a reputation as one of the leading producers of electronic musicians in the world today. After ten years of cutting edge electronica, Electric Skychurch is still going strong.

For more info on Electric Skychurch, check out: **www.electricskychurch.com**.

What are you working on at the moment?
JL: I'm working on a new single for myself and I just finished off two Remixes. One is the song Whole Lot of Love by Led Zepplin. I ended up using the Electrix Warp Factory and made the whole thing into a kind of dirty sex song. I went back to the original Led Zepplin song and it's basically about sex on acid so I did a sort of James Brown American deep groove thing with a talking bass guitar. And I've just finished a Remix of a Bob Marley song called Mr. Brown. I've been asked to Remix a lot of rock bands lately and I've become kind of known for that.

So does every pop star want dance Remixes that can be played in clubs?
JL: No, every pop star's record label wants a dance Remix to help keep selling that pop star. It's a straight-up business deal.

How do the pop stars feel about that?

Well, I live in Hollywood and a lot of these people are my neighbors. When I go down the street to get Mexican food, these are the people I see. A lot of the rock guys I run into say that they hear a dance Remix and think that it's cool but it's missing the point of the song. What I do is try to figure out what the little tiny nugget of meaning that can not be lost and take that one little thing - maybe a riff or one piece of a vocal - toss the rest out and then build a new song up from that point and try to hold on to what the song is about throughout the Remix. If you can pull that off a couple of times then you start to get calls.

Do you usually get the calls from the record companies or the musicians?

JL: The record companies and the bands. Or sometimes a smaller dance label might be doing a Remix project for another record company. I get calls from everybody but I really like getting calls from the artists because then I get a chance to talk to them about the song. Gong from England called me last year and asked me to do a Remix. They sent me copies of their 24 track masters from the seventies and I fell in love with this stuff. So I assume that, for this track, I'm a member of Gong. So I cut it up and put it back together and sent it to them. They loved it and the next time they were in LA they took me out and told me that I had captured the soul of Gong. That was the highest compliment I could get and it was also the best Remix I ever did.

Is there sometimes pressure from the record company to do a more commercial kind of dance mix?

JL: I've never had anybody ask me for anything specific. If you are going to do a Remix and there's five other people working on it, you can pretty much guarantee that all of the overwrought styles around today will be represented. I'm not interested in doing the latest, greatest, popular mix around. I'm more interested in taking the track, turning it inside out and painting it a different color.

There has always been a dichotomy between the creative and the technical, and a point at which the technology becomes more of a hindrance than a help to the creative process.

JL: Yes, that definitely happened to me a couple of years ago. It was great leaning the technology down to the microprocessor level, but once you've mastered it, you are left with pure expression. What's happened for me is that these electronic gizmos started out being musical instruments, then became pure technology, and now it's coming back around to being pure

Remix: The Electronic Music Explosion

expression. For the Bob Marley Remix I am working on I am using a Mac G3 in place of a sampler running a hard disc recorder and then I'll use something to take the digital edge off of it like a Roland space echo or an analogue filter and maybe an old Juno. I may have a studio full of equipment but on one song I'll probably only use a computer, a couple of vintage effects processors and maybe two synths. That's all you really need. You can do a great Remix with a four-track and a set of decks. In the end it comes down to you more than the gear. But the gear makes it a lot easier!

What do you mean by "the digital edge?"
JL: A good way to describe it is to compare it with video games. If you look at an old video game you can see the image is made up of little blocks that make jagged lines. With digital you are listening to that jagged line and the better the gear, the smother the line. When I look for gear I'm looking for smooth. You can always make it jagged if you want that but you can't make it smoother.

What are the considerations when choosing software over hardware?
JL: I don't thing that the computer-based stuff is really there yet. Computers are a great interface with the gear that you already have. When I'm remixing I use my computer for an interface with the samplers I already have. I use the computer to digitally load all the information that I need. If some one gives me a DAT tape to Remix and it's five minutes of audio and some disembodied voices or whatever, I'll load that into my computer and chop it up really fast and then shoot it down the wire into the samplers and start working on it in a more traditional way. The computer is supposed to do everything but, in reality, it doesn't do one thing really well. I've also found that the more applications you are running on the computer, the more time you are going to spend making sure that the computer is still running. One of the biggest complaints that I hear is, "I'm a musician and not a computer technician" and people are spending a lot of time keeping their computers running. Things like cleaning off the hard drive, checking for viruses, updating and debugging software. I've spent months on this bullshit and there's a lot to be said for sitting down at a keyboard with a built in sequencer that works the same way every day and doesn't crash. I once did an entire recording session that completely failed because of a timing synchronization bug in the software and we lost a month's worth of work. The thing was so fast that the MIDI port couldn't keep up with the music so we had to go out and buy a Yamaha table top sequencer which ran better than

the computer. I've talked to the guys at Steinberg Jones who make Q-base and they did bench testing with different interfaces and got wildly different results. The new USB standard—a new interface standard for computers—will hopefully make it a little more solid in the future. At the moment, if you are doing a lot of really fast work, then I would recommend dumping it into a dedicated machine that doesn't have to worry about drawing a picture on a screen. You might also find that you like the sound a little better.

What computer programs do you use regularly?
JL: I use Q-Base, Audio VST 24, Bias Peak. I also use Galaxy, Synthesizer Librarian, and Recycle. What I usually do is load stuff into Peak from DAT, chop it up, recycle it and then load it into my samplers and then sequence it with Q-Base. Once I get it the way I like it, I'll start recording long passages of analogue synthesizers and finally do a digital mix down of all the material and archive it on CD ROM. At the end of a project I have a CD that contains digital copies of the analogue tracks, copies of all the synthesizer data and copies if all of the sequence files. And I mix it all down through an analogue Soundcraft desk.

Could you walk us through a typical method you would use for a Remix?
JL: You always start with a kernel or seed from the original piece of music. For the Bob Marley track I'm working on, they sent me a tape with vocals on it that were extracted from the original master tapes. I take that vocal and I find one loop I like. In this case it's the lines, "Mr. Brown is a clown, that rides around town in a coffin." I take that one loop and load it into a sampler. And it doesn't need to be a twenty-thousand dollar piece of hardware, this can be your old Ensoniq from 1988. So I'll loop the sample and find a tempo I like or I might use the sampler to change the tempo and the pitch. Then I'll use the same sampler to write drum grooves along with maybe a drum machine. So now we have a sampler and a drum machine and a tape somebody gave me. And I might work on that loop an entire day to find the right groove. Then I'll zoom out and use a computer to start arranging that groove and use some effects units to change the original vocal sample to give it a certain tone. Finally, I'll use a synthesizer to glue it all together and you have a Remix.

What pieces of equipment would you recommend to someone who wants to start making tracks?

JL: The first thing I tell people is look around and see what you've got because you may have what you need already. If you have a computer, you can go out and get freeware or shareware demo software and play with it. A computer may not be the most Hi-Fi way to go but it's a good start. I started out with an old Ensoniq sampler with a built-in sequencer and I did loads of mixes and Remixes on that alone. A good pair of headphones, a master keyboard that samples, and a desire to do it is all you really need. I did a mix last year for a movie called Pi, a track called Full Moon Generator. I was on tour and I did it in a hotel room with a K 2000, a Mackie 12-02 and a set of headphones and it turned out to be the best work I did that year.

So it's the musical ideas that make the track rather than the technology?

JL: Exactly. The technology will always be a component because even if you just sing into a microphone, you need a microphone, a pre-amp and a tape deck.

Would you agree that a lot of the new electronic music has been created by people who found new ways of using the existing technology?

JL: Yes, a good example is the Roland TB 303 and the TR 606. These machines were originally intended to simulate a bass guitar and a drummer so that you could have backing tracks for your demos. Nobody ever intended for the 303 to become this iconic acid house instrument. That was never part of the plan. It was marketed to straight-up rock and roll musicians. The interesting thing about electronic instruments is that they are usually released as toys and it's the people who use them that find a niche for them and turn them into instruments over time.

Do you find that with keyboards with so many pre-sets there is a danger of overusing them and sounding the same as everyone else?

JL: If you go and buy any keyboard there is always a bunch of demo junk programmed into it, like the rave/Casio sounds in the groove boxes. But if you go in there and rip all that stuff out you will find something that that machine can do that no other machine can do. That's what's cool about it, but it's up to you to find it. Style can be a real trap. When drum and bass first emerged as its own style, I was really excited about it because the use of the tools had evolved. The tools didn't create drum and bass, it's the people using the tools and sharing information that develops a style. I don't think that the founders of drum and bass set out to invent drum and bass, it just evolved over time. And then someone has to come in and start over again with new ideas.

Is there a tend towards using more organic sounds in electronic mixes?
JL: We go out with field recorders and collect sounds. It's something that the computer is really good for. One of the things that has happened with electronic music is, people use samples and make a track, then the track gets sampled and so on until this audio is five or six generations down the road and it gets flat and looses its dynamic range. If you go back and listen to Dark Side of the Moon or some classical music, you are blown away by how much depth and detail there is in the recording. So you wonder how to get that depth back into your recordings and the answer is to get a microphone, record some stuff and put it into the background of your electronic track. That will create a depth and ambiance behind the beats and really helps to open it up.

What are the most exciting new developments in electronic music technology?
JL: Cheap hard disk recording. If you are using samplers, one of the big limitations is memory. Samplers really lend them selves to drums because a drum hit takes up a small portion of memory. A hard disk recorder can record a four minute passage of music, like a slowly evolving synthesizer passage that's never the same twice. All of a sudden, a producer with an $899 iMac has the ability to record a studio quality vocal track, bass track or even a sound effect track. So it can take electronic music one step away from the loop and focus on arrangement and composition a little bit differently. I think that cheap hard disc recorders will bridge the gap between electronic music and so-called "real" music. The successful hybrid artists are the ones with access to high end technology. Like the stuff from New York where they take a full orchestra and put minimal beats behind it. Everyone will be able to do that soon.

How did you get into electronic music coming from a background as bass player?
JL: Well, I was a synth player before I was a bass player. My first Synth was a Juno 106, which I bought new when it was released back in 1983. It's still my main keyboard.

I played bass in funk bands, so the transition back and forth from guitars to synth and drum machines was transparent. Guitars, drums, drum machines and synths are all still part of my sound, except now I use more samples of recordings I make in the studio.

My big jump away from bass playing and into techno occurred back in 1991. I shattered my left hand in a freak roller-rave accident, so my 'shedding days came to an end and my programming got better fast.

Many people start out feel that equipment is the key to making an impact. In reality, great compositions can come from very simple rigs. What was your earliest electronic rig?
JL: A Juno 106, and a Roland Cube-60 keyboard amp. I was making ambient music with it. Now, I still use the 106 as my main instrument, but I don't really favor the amp. I like a good set of floor monitors.

Can you describe your current studio set up VS you road rig?
JL: I find having two identical sets of gear impractical. It just makes things harder to play out live, so I tend to use my live rig for composition.

I travel with a TB-303, two Juno 106's, a MKS-50, a JD-990 and an R-8 MKII. I also take two Kurzweil K2000 samplers (a keyboard for synths and a rack for drums), a Novation Drumstation for my classic 808 and 909 drum machine sounds. I use a Yamaha QY-700 as a sequencer (I do not use computers onstage – they are too unpredictable, and offer little interaction with the music live) For live FX I use three units by Electrix, the Warp Factory, Filter Factory, and MoFX. I also use a Roland SDE-330 delay and a bunch of cheap compressors. I do not mix onstage, so all of my keyboards and sound modules are submixed down to 24 outputs and sent to a big front-of-house console.

All of my gear is seriously thrashed - when something has been repaired over 10 times, I'll generally replace it and put the wobbly unit in the studio. I have a lot of dead machines, and I keep them around for spare parts. I can fix my own stuff, and have fixed my K2000 rack at least 20 times. That one is a trooper. United Airlines destroyed my original JD-990 – the guys at Roland were laughing at me when I brought it in for the last time. I also cracked the circuit boards on my MC-202 and TR-606, those units sorta work but don't travel with me anymore.

I attempted to travel with a digital board, but it broke the first time it flew on a plane. I took that as a bad sign and went back to analog.

There are a couple of things that stay in the studio, such as a G3 Mac that I use for audio recording, A to D converters, and vintage tape delays. I also keep a bunch of analog synths that are too old to travel with which include an Arp Omni, a Roland RS-202, MC-202, SH-101, TR-606, a Moog Realistic, and a Sequential Circuits Pro-1. All this stuff is patched in through various submixers into my hard disk recorder for sampling and live tracking. There are lots of compressors and effects units, too numerous to mention.

On top of all of that, I maintain a nice collection of microphones, guitars, basses, and hand drums. I rarely record a track without playing something live, even if that live instrument only exists as a sample.

I had a big vanity console in my studio, but sold it because I needed the floor space, and would rather have a couch.

A few years back I tried to make a soundproof mixing environment, and discovered renting world class rooms for the mix is cheaper in the long run. Sounds better, too. My studio is for recording only, which I do with a Mac, Vintage Neve Pre Amps and Apogee converters.

Often a remixer starts with raw vocals that have been removed from the master and dubbed onto DAT tape. How do you begin the process with your Remixes?
JL: I always start by listening to the artist's original song. I figure, if I do it right, I can capture the artist's original emotional intent without railroading my "style" over the song.

Next, I'll dump the DAT tape into my computer for faster editing. From there, I'll take what I feel to be the "hook" from the song, and load it into my samplers.

Do you have a set idea before you begin or is it more organic and experimental process as the piece develops?
JL: When I set a "goal" things rarely work out, so instead I take that one little sample as the "soul" of the piece, and then I use my live performance rig to start composing the music around it. Generally, I'll start with melodies—most DJ producers start with

Remix: The Electronic Music Explosion

beats. Then I'll work up the harmonic structure of the piece and the changes, and then finally I'll work out the skeleton of the drums. I prefer to work this way because I like making drum kits that fit in with the tone of the music.

If you were stranded on a desert island which piece of gear would you most want to have with you?
JL: My Juno 106! With a solar panels, of course.

How did Electric Skychurch come about?
JL: Well, way back in 1989 I lived in Athens, Georgia and was playing bass in a funk band called "The Groove Trolls." At the time, I was really into acid house, and I wanted to incorporate drum machines into the act. My idea was that everybody, including the live drummer, could play along to a heavy "909" kick. The Trolls busted up, and I pursued the drum machine idea by myself using the name "Electric Skychurch."

I worked on demos alone for a long time, and released a solo cassette in Los Angeles in 1991. A couple of friends had a vending table at raves, where they sold the first Skychurch cassettes.

I took on band members from 1992 through 1994, put out some proper records and began playing out now and then. Eventually everything just blew up and I was on the road continuously from 1996 until 1999.

How does Skychurch differ from what you envisioned early on?
JL: Skychurch was conceived as a live performance project and it is that, but I never realized just how big it would get. The music, and I'm specifically talking about composition, has become more detailed and personal than I originally imagined. I went through a period of pouring my heart out, and then found myself frightened by how personal my music had become to other people. So what started out as a "band" ended up as a forum for communication, on a gut level, with other people.

Instead of trying to come up with the next big DJ style (which I feel is a competitive trap) I've come around to basic songwriting —simple communication though music. Electronic gadgets are my instruments of choice, but I could just as easily play piano and sing to get my point across.

It's not about the gear, it's about what you and I have in common.

How does your current roster differ from the original Skychurch?
JL: Skychurch was originally a primitive solo project that became a band, and then went through many changes, and then finally blossomed back into a mature solo project.

I come from "live" bands and have learned the hard way that electronic music is just not a "band" paradigm. In live music, everyone has to work together in order to make it; however, in electronic music everyone can go off and make a record on their laptop. So take all the normal drama of a rock band and amplify that with the "screw you I'm gonna do it myself" attitude of punk rock, and mix in some cheap hard disk recording and you have a new paradigm.

This is a fundamental change in the social structure of music. As soon as an electronic band has a taste of success, the members usually go off in different directions. You may notice that most electronic bands have no more than 2 members. It's too bad, because I really believe that the interaction between people can be very interesting.

The positive way out in this situation seems to be the "session." Lately I've been really happy to host guest sessions with different friends and musicians. I really have fun inviting someone over to play on a track, even if they will never tour with me. It helps me get out of my own head and freshens up the music.

I just finished a string of successful "Back to Basics" solo shows. Skychurch is back to what it was in the beginning! After 16 years of hard work, I find myself standing in front of a Juno 106 singing into a microphone, which is exactly what I was doing in my parent's basement when I was 16 years old. How funny! Now I'm 32 and I've spent half my life just to get back to where I started!

Who were some of your early influences in electronic music?
JL: Brian Eno, Laurie Anderson, Devo, Kraftwerk, Thomas Dolby, early OMD, Jean Michel Jarre.

Electronic Music and culture seem to be moving from underground to mainstream with more and more producers incorporating dance production into POP music. How do you think this will effect so called underground music?
JL: I think this is nothing new, just part of the continuing evolution of thought.

If you were doing this hard, minimal electronic music in the '80s you were a freak. There was no money in it. There was no tradition. You just did it because you loved the sound of it. There were other types of electronic music out there, but not as much as we are swamped with today.

Electronic pop music was there in the late '80s. It was Madonna and the Pet Shop Boys, and it still is. The difference is now the tools are affordable, so everyone can make tracks. And when everyone can participate in something, it becomes popular, which is what pop is all about.

Now you can put together a track with preset sounds, grooves and sample CDs. You never have to get into the music at the note for note level. Sometimes that's great, unfortunately people tend to imitate each other much too closely, especially in the commercial music world. When money is on the line, people tend to go with what is already proven as popular.

So pop music starts with the popularization of an underground form, which leads to the commercialization of similar forms. In our case the electric guitar has given way to the sequencer form, but the commercial intent behind the music has remained the same.

Underground music will always evolve into something different. The underground is there because it fulfills people's desire for novelty and emotional authenticity. That's why drum and bass rose up at the same time the techno sound palette was turned over to the Spice Girls. It has always been this way.

Surviving in this industry often means wearing a number of hats. How many do you wear?
JL: Primarily just one songwriter. But also entertainer, performer, musician, producer, technician, heavy lifter, bass player, and ex-party animal turned introspective.

How long does it typically take you to complete a Remix?
JL: About a week. Even if I nail it in one day, I keep it on the board for a week just to make sure I like it.

What happens if a client doesn't like your Remix?
JL: I don't have a lot of time to do Remixes, so I pick them very carefully. I would rather Remix rock bands because it's more fun. I did Bob Marley last year. You can't screw up Bob Marley – it's so good to begin with. It was a blast!

I usually don't do "dance floor" Remixes. I'm not a DJ, and I don't think like one. I'm known for doing Remixes that work well on radio, and they turn up on TV all the time.

Once I have had a record company think my Remix was too esoteric, but fortunately the artist championed the mix for other reasons. The mix, which was a trip-hop Version of "Mad World" by the Zen Cowboys, ended up as the theme song for an HBO special. Go figure.

You are releasing a new piece entitled Heaven. Can you tell us about it and where you see it fitting into the market?
JL: Well, that's a funny one. I did that on the fly in a few years ago. It's a love song for my wife. I would have released it back then, but we had a little professional detour.

I had a nasty conflict with my old record company over my contract, and so "Heaven" sat in the can for a few years. When the conflict started easing up, I had hundreds of demos lying around. I gave the demos to my closest DJ friends, and that was the song everyone wanted. I was surprised!

It really stands alone as a track in a style that has yet to be labeled. It's very popular, and I never really thought it would be so *important* to so many people.

I put it on my website as a free MP3, so most people have emailed their friends a copy. It's my own little positive computer virus. You can grab a copy at **http://www.skychurch.com**.

Where do you see the dance culture in 5 years from now?
JL: Hmmmm... I think you will see a backlash against "dance" that has nothing to do with "electronic," although the two will be confused.

Perhaps the emphasis on "dance floor" will give way to other forms of electronic music. Different time signatures, ambient soundscapes, electronic vocal music, electro-punk, or whatever anyone may dream up.

In my opinion the "dance floor" part of electronic music is the most rigid and stagnant part of "dance" culture. It's great for DJ's, but it forces artists into a corner, so expect a major rebellion on that point alone.

What kind of impact are MP3 files having on the industry?
JL: MP3 is the college radio of the 21st century. I think the average kid that would have taped music off of the radio will get music for free off the net. This inevitably cuts back on the amount of new commercial music someone is willing to purchase.

The industry will have to rethink itself, because the current infrastructure just can't maintain itself without heavy cash flow. Sooner or later someone will figure out how to make a buck at e-music, and it will be interesting to see who comes out on top.

MP3's make it easier for artists to promote themselves by giving away free music, but they have to make money elsewhere to survive. Entertaining a crowd—playing concerts—becomes more important.

Amateur music will become significant as the means of distribution becomes cheaper, and I expect to see a lot of websites that sort through the stuff for you picking the best tracks out of the avalanche of new music—just like college radio.

Is Electronica here to stay?
JL: Electronic Music is part of our culture, and will change without disappearing entirely. The term "Electronica" may fall out of favor the way "disco" did back in the early '80s—but disco never really died, it just became something else.

Let's identify electronic music by singling out two musical techniques. We can identify it from either its synthetic sound palette or the use of sequencers. Electronic music has been around since the 1960s, and we have only recently recognized it, in retrospect, as its own form.

The names we use to identify electronic music will definitely change, but electronic music is already a part of history, just like jazz and rock.

Fig. #43: Steve Stoll

PHOTO: STEVE SULLIVAN

Steve Stoll is an anomaly. Acknowledged worldwide as a leading techno-crat, Steve has a varied background as producer, musician and DJ. Stoll is well known for his pure, minimalist analogue-minded techno productions in the vein of early Plastikman and Joey Beltram.

Raised in Brooklyn N.Y., Steve listened to hip-hop and disco as a child, then joined the Army straight out of high school. He served for five years, including a period in the Gulf War when he plotted bomb runs by satellite. After being released, he shifted around: he played drums for the industrial group Sister Machine Gun, studied jazz and began recording straight-edged techno for Big Apple labels like 212 Productions and Damon Wild's Synewave. Debuting with his Pacemaker album in 1995, Stoll went on to record for Nova Mute, Probe, DJax, Delirium, Synewave and his own Proper NYC label. He recorded for Zero

Divide (as the Operator) and made an EP for Nova Mute (as the Blunted Boy Wonder). After he reverted back to Steve Stoll, Damn Analog Technology followed in 1997 and The Blunted Boy Wonder one year later.

Steve, you started out your musical career as a drummer and went on to play with the industrial group Sister Machine Gun. How did you make the transition to a hard-hitting techno producer and DJ?
SS: I actually felt that this was a very smooth transition as my interest in electronics, sampling, and so forth went back many years before my involvement with Wax Trax. I always wanted to take my role as a "beat writer" and programmer and expand it into the role of producer. I've always approached my music very much as a drummer. For me the beat is always first and last in a production. In fact, synthesizers and samplers have always been percussion instruments to me as I often program them from percussion controllers. Sometimes it's all about looking at things in a different way and playing up to your limitations.

You mentioned that you recently converted your studio to Mac G3-based software after years of using primarily hardware sampler/sequencers. Would you first describe your old set up and then explain the new set up. Why the change?
SS: Although I've been running Logic for many years I really only used it for doing Remixes and the occasional track. I have always been much more comfortable to use my hardware sequencer (mpc-200) as it was the way that I learned to write tracks, and as we get set in our ways in the studio it's sometimes hard to break old habits. I finally decided that I needed to rethink my whole set up and got the upgrade to Logic Platinum and I haven't looked back. I have become a convert to doing everything in the Mac and the dsp effects are amazing. I must admit that for synth programming I still prefer to be hands on, but I can't help but think how programs that take sequencing a step further are changing the way we write music. I really think were only a few years away from the entire studio being on a micro-processor that you'll be able to carry around in your pocket.

Every producer has a favorite "secret weapon" that they use in the studio that is ultimately associated with their sound. Without letting too much out of the bag, would you give us an idea of your arsenal?
SS: If I answered this they wouldn't be secret weapons any more! I recently I had a producer come up to me in Holland and say "man, I got all your sounds, I just got a Waldorf Pulse". I guess I've always been associated with a pretty agressive analog sound,

I've always been a fan of the Sequential Pro One, I've been using them on tracks for some time now. Also, the Pulse is very intuitive for me and has got a very quick attack which is very esential in a synth for me. I think ultimately though the gear is second to the ideas in your head. I know guys with much bigger so-called better studios that never had an original idea. I like to think that no matter what you have in front of you the sound should be "yours."

How do you approach a Remix verses an original production? Do you have a particular beat or bass line in mind, a standard way of arranging?

SS: Remixing has always been a bit of a dark horse for me as my logical mind always thinks, if the track is so good why bother to Remix it? I also am a firm believer in sticking many elements of the original in the mix, and not simply writing a new track and calling it a Remix, I think that as well as not being a Remix, this is an insult to the artist who is paying for the mix. Occasionally I do get different approaches to Remixing which seem to work out. A technique that I recently used on a Remix was to load the main loop of the original into Logic Audio then convert it to MIDI. This is a very slick way of using all of my own sounds while using the exact sequence of the original. Overall I would say it's harder for me to think up a different approach to Remix a track than to create an original. I guess this is why a lot of guys who only Remix get stuck in a formula for doing them.

Who were some of your early influences?

SS: When I was young I was heavily into Gary Numan, Public Enemy, all the great jazz drummers, and my grandfather who used to play them to me. I think you have to be like a sponge and kind of absorb all different musical influences. I can find points that I like in pretty much all music.

Your career seems to have developed in Europe faster than in the US. Do you think this is the case with many North American artists?

SS: I think this had a lot to do with the fact that Europe was feeling techno years before the States. Although the origins of the music are very firmly rooted in The States, none of us were feeling the love in America. I've always thought that this was a reflection of the "guitar mentality" that prevails here, although I see that very rapidly changing as more and more rock bands are being influenced by dance music. Kids coming up now really seem to be gravitating toward dj rigs, samplers, and synths as opposed to only having the option in the past of either playing bass, guitar, or drums. Over the years I've kind of realized that the producer as an artist may still a strange concept to Americans but I just accept the way things are at this point and I'm very happy to be able to travel the world.

Does any of the "live" mixing feel get lost with an automated mix?
SS: I have always been against the automated or computer mixing. For me it's always been very important to be hands on during mixdown whether it be a studio session or a DJ mix. I have always been a fan of live misic and the mixing desk is how you convey that with techno. Growing up with jazz I realized the importance of having the ability to be spontaneous and for me live mixing is the only way. Little pops, clicks, and other "mistakes" like that make the music much more exciting for me.

You have successfully recorded on many labels including your own Proper NYC and most recently on 212 productions. What is the relationship between the two and why have more than one label?
SS: Having a very prolific output was the main motivation for starting Proper. I was also getting sick of the politics of working with outside labels. I wanted to be able to control the release schedule and more importantly if I had something to put out that I believed in I was free to really go for it. Starting the sub-label 212 Productions was done as I was working on very hard tracky stuff that I felt didn't fit necessarily on Proper but was still worthy of coming out. The 212 stuff was very underground, minimal label info and in fact, all the new 212 projects only have catalog numbers and you can check the website listed on the label if you want more info and production notes.

Although you primarily DJ when you tour, you mentioned that you will be booking some "live PA" shows in the near future. What is your preference?
SS: For many years I only PAed. The reason for the return to DJing was kind of two-fold. Firstly I seemed to be getting plagued by technical problems in '98 and I was starting to feel that it was time to make a change. Some gigs can be approached with an underground mentality but playing in front of 20,000 people without sound check is a reality check. Secondly, I really enjoy playing much longer sets than my typical one hour PA and DJing gives me the freedom to play...5 hours if I need to. At this point I can't say that I prefer one over the other. I do find it very satisfying to DJ. However, I really am looking forward to getting back on the road with the live rig again.

When you are playing live you use the Akai MPC as the engine for your sets. What other equipment do you use on stage?

SS: This is something that was almost changing from gig to gig for me in the early days. As many live acts know this is a limitation of space and what you can hump to the airport almost more than anything else. Currently the parts of my live rig that stay consistent are: The Akai MPC as the master sequencer, The Roland 909 and, Roland R8-mk2 (the most underrated drum machine ever made), Electrix Filter Factory (the best live hands-on filterbank ever). With this very basic setup I can recreate any one of my tracks for a live performance and have the ability to change the length, patterns, and effects at will.

Your use of big reverb and delay gives some of your tracks a certain "dub" feel. Are you influenced by this sound?

SS: I am a huge fan of dub and in fact I sometimes play King Tubby and Scientist tracks to get in the mood to mix. I have recently got a tape delay and I'm really loving that feedback! Dub for me is so very close to techno, as is hip-hop, jazz, classical. I can really feel it in almost every type of music I hear. But the "misuse" of gear in dub was something that I have always been feeling.

Although your tracks have a definite techno sound, It seems that there is also a funk feel to some of them. Do you think we will see a resurgence of funk in modern dance production or will it remain a straight 4/4 rhythm?

SS: We always define our music by rhythm. Techno and house have always been defined by a 4/4 kick pattern much in the same way that jazz is defined by the 3/4 ride cymbal swing pattern. I think it is very interesting to be able to play over these defined patterns and really create something that works musically. I mean as a drummer I hate things that don't swing, just because we are playing with machines doesn't mean we can't give them a kick in the ass and make something funky come out of these boxes. It's all about how deep you go with your gear, you really have to get inside of how something is programmed and rip it apart. That's techno!

Where do you see the dance market five years from know? What are the current trends?

SS: I think it's a mistake to try to see where things will be in five years.

It's all changing so fast. One thing is certain in the music business; it will never stop evolving or changing. I think that as humans we have to also do the same thing always be open to new ideas and constantly evolving. There is a saying from Kerouac which goes "submissive to everything, open, listening." I think that sums it up.

How do you spit your time between traveling and studio work?
SS: It has almost gotten to be a bit routine over the years, but I leave for Europe on Friday, play on Saturday, return to New York on Sunday, jet lag on Monday, and work in the studio the rest of the week. I get a lot of musical ideas from traveling so I'm always a bit anxious to get the studio turned on when I return home.

It seems that kids all over the world aspire to be DJs and ultimately Remixers. Can you offer any sage words of advice to someone who is just starting out?
SS: The best advice I can offer would be not to rush things. I really believe if you work hard and push yourself you can develop ideas and a sound people will want to hear. I know it's really cliche sounding but this is what I know to be true. Oh yeah, have a good publisher from the beginning!

INTERVIEW WITH DERRICK PERKINS

Fig. #44: Derrick Perkins Photo

Associate Producer and programmer on Stevie Wonder's two time GRAMMY® Award winning Hit "For Your Love," Platinum Producer Derrick Perkins Owes it all to Full Sail's *Real World Education.*

Derrick Perkins, a Florida based producer, songwriter, programmer and remixer, has worked with many industry giants including Stevie Wonder and Elton John. Additionally, Derek has extensive credits in television/film soundtrack production including producing Michael Jordan's recent TV commercial for his Jordan clothing line featuring Mary J. Blige in a remake of a classic Stevie Wonder song.

As if this isn't enough to keep him busy, Derrick still finds time to teach at the world-renowned Full Sail Recording Academy in Orlando, Florida. A new program, headed by Perkins, is the first of its kind to offer courses geared toward dance production and up-and-coming DJs, producers, and remixers. Graduates of Full Sail are virtually guaranteed a place in the industry due to their highly regarded programs.

We caught up to Derrick in his car while on the way rewire Visio Sonic's studio in Tampa.

You have had a very diverse career in studio production, engineering and programming. You mentioned that recently there has been a shift in the type of students interested in Full Sail and that many have a DJ background. Do you see this trend continuing to grow?
DP: "Yes, many of our new students are interested in the DJ style production, whether they are actual DJs or not. Albums produced by DJs or DJ compilation projects are becoming an ever-growing trend, hitting artists like Cher and Madonna who have put the limelight on this style. Other labels, producers and artists say "Humm?? I need to incorporate this into my sound to stay competitive." So, DJs are seeing the potential of making a career for themselves like any other producer if they can learn the full gambit of the industry.

It seems that many pop releases these days will feature a number of Remixed versions to give the track more potential and hopefully get it across in other markets. Do you get into talking about multiple Remixes of a release in your class?

DP: Yea, that was one of the most joyful things of my career when I graduated in 1989. remixing was something that was starting to get a lot of attention and then when that whole hip-hop, break dancing, urban culture thing began to blow up it brought a lot of attention to DJs who were doing simplified versions of pop tracks or 'flipping' them or using the chorus and rapping to them.

How does a Remix studio differ from a regular recording studio?

DP: A Remix studio is usually a stripped-down, simplified recording studio. It usually consists of samplers, hardware or software sequencers, tone modules and effects. All of these things can fit into a relatively small un-treated room that doesn't require the acoustics of a traditional recording studio. When you're working on a Remix, the vocal is already compete and the song already has at least one established style. The whole purpose is to put the artist into another genre of music. For example, you can take a country/pop song and make it accessible and likeable in the dance market. To build a studio at home using today's technology is easy to do. Material usually comes in on a DAT tape or as a Pro Tools file depending on your weapon of choice. Usually by the Remix stage, the material is all in the digital domain and you are going direct into your computer or hardware sampler where you can assemble and make your arrangement. I find that I do most production in various home studios and then we do the final mixing and sweetening in bigger, more expensive studios where we may need the acoustic qualities of a room.

So, typically when you get a Remix job do you get say a dry vocal on a DAT or do you have access to more elements?

DP: When I'm working with a label, I will typically listen to the original to see if there are any elements or no elements that I want to keep. Sometimes I'll just take a part with the intention of re-voicing. Say if there is a horn line, I might decide to turn it to a vocal line. This is what I did with the "Brand New Heavies" on the Brother-Sister Remix. It kind of turned into an acid jazzy instrumental as opposed to a vocal oriented R&B or hip-hop. These guys are great singers and players in the old school R&B style but the Remix took them into a whole new market that they wouldn't have normally touched. This is an example of why Remixing is such a powerful technique. Today remixers take most pride in totally creating a new piece of music that the original vocals fit into.

So, I guess if you are working with the label, you can have a pick of the parts that are on the original multitrack? Will you typically dump the tracks that you have selected into a digital audio workstation or a hard disk recorder?

DP: Yea, this is the idea. Many of today's programs enable you to lock your MIDI and digital audio tracks. Most people are using this technique although some still like to use external sequencers like the Akai MPC. It all depends on what you're most comfortable with. Often it's a combination of old school hardware tools and computer programs. There's really no right or wrong way to do things, as long as the product sounds good in the end.

It seems that more and more the Remix producer is being sought after by record companies, publishers and studios. What is the difference between a remixer and a traditional studio guy?

DP: Well, it's really a cultural thing. I'm from the culture of all these weird toys and unorthodox tools and ways of doing things with music. A traditional producer will use traditional style instruments. Electronic instruments are not played like traditional instruments as their range and scale can be dramatically changed. This is the advantage you have with a sampler. All the windows are being pushed and the DJ is another level on top of all this, turntables plus all these electronic tools. They save time and it enables you to do it at home.

It seems that a lot of the successful remixers have had backgrounds as DJs. Is this because they inherently understand what makes people want because they have had first hand experience trying to get people to dance in a club?

DP: I think that's true but there is a danger of generalizing dance music you know there's all kinds of tempos and cues that come into play. You could generalize and say that we can all dance from 95bpm on up. This thought is not accurate enough and does not take the DJ's intuitive skills into play. It's all about timing. I went to watch Sasha and I realized that he had timing down to an art form. Timing when the set was going to peak, when the club would close. It's a lot of control, almost like directing an orchestra with vinyl.

It would seem that many elements of dance production are finding their way into mainstream music. For example, loops are becoming more popular and many pop songs feature Roland 909 drums, filters, vocoders, etc. What are students looking to learn from you these days? What kind of equipment interests them?

DP: You know it's funny you say that 'cause it kind of bridges your last question when you asked me what attracted me to dance stuff when I was the age of my students. You know one thing that attracted me was the vocoder. You know Roger Troutman, God rest his soul, who just formally passed? I remember when they used to bring him in and the ticket was to watch him play over 20-25 instruments on stage during his whole set. But what made him was the level to which he established the vocoder. You know, Stevie Wonder probably used it first but Roger made it part of his everyday show. He kind of made a comeback with the Dr. Dre and the Tupac track and a lot of stuff out on the West Coast, DJ Quick, and it started to leak out with people doing Remixes using his vocoder tracks. A lot of this type of stuff is currently coming from Europe. Check out that new track "Blue." People like the vocoder in combination with dance tracks. DJs are using it as a new instrument in Electronica. You know, especially when you can give it (the vocoder) 8 or 16 bars in the arrangement. You can take the track to a whole new level. Vocoders, synchronized delays, tremelos and things like that work really well when you can set it to eighth notes or sixteenth notes, it creates a lot of versatility in a track. Many people are doing this sort of thing in mixing these days. You don't want to let a mix just sit there. People want the thing moving. They want alive. You don't want to let an eight bar or sixteen bar just sit. You want to color it, make it move, make it spicy.

Vocoder Spotlight

Innovative funkster Roger Troutman was the master of the vocoder—a keyboard synthesizer that created robotic-sounding vocals through the simultaneous use of a piano-like interface and a breath controller (breath tube); somewhat like a guitar talk box. What James Jamerson did for the bass, Jimi Hendrix for the guitar and Stevie Wonder for the harmonica, Troutman did for the vocoder. As member of Zapp!, a band that included his brothers Larry, Lester and Tony Troutman and recording under the solo moniker of Roger, he helped define and give personality to a difficult-to-play instrument that previously was

used for gimmicky effects. With his winning smile and charming playfulness, Troutman was a favorite on stage and record. He'd often bring his vocoder along on radio interviews, treating the listeners to his amazing vocoder skills.
Ed Hogan—All Music Guide

We see a great deal of dance production making its way into pop music these days. Do you think that there is a danger of dance music becoming too commercialized?

DP: I think that it is dangerous for DJs. It's a big industry and great creative ideas are only one element of what it takes. You have to be able to hold a record in your hand and know how it was produced and what stages it took to get it to that point. From the point of conception, you know what I'm saying'? Oh, here's this song "Bye Bye Baby" Ok? I have this, we're hitting two sticks together. Now how do I get to the point of walking into a concert or an arena to do a performance of that song for thirty thousand? They need to know how it gets to that point. Not necessarily it in terms of how to show it and do it maybe but at least in understanding it because that's the music they're taking and calling it their own. The danger of walking into this industry without knowing how to do certain things and to get certain sounds like the album that they've been playing for so many years. Getting some form of education prevents that danger. Any enthusiast of any style of music will always fight to keep it real and close to its roots. There's a lot of people who aren't part of the dance culture or the Electronica culture that will always use and abuse certain forms. You know Hollywood tends to always hire one arranger for whatever style of music is called for. I've been in to replace some of them. They'll try to hire one composer who they think is going to create electronic music when he's not part of that culture and doesn't even go to clubs or monitor the scene. They'll always try to simulate anything that is popular but the real thing will always come through.

So I guess you could say that there's more to it than the sound of the 909 or a filter or what ever, it's about inherently understanding what to do with these tools?

DP: Exactly. We teach the WarpFactory or Mo-FX or what ever but we will go on to teach the concepts of delay so it's not just a word to them. We'll show them tape delay for example, open reel tape delay with two tape machines. It's kind of teaching past present and future.

What is the best way for a DJ to start familiarizing himself with the studio mentality?

DP: I think that every DJ should take a basic music theory class. Take a basic recording and engineering class and a basic MIDI digital audio course. Almost any community college offers this type of course. Watch for workshops or look into private schools that will offer this type of program but get some training one way or the other. Even music stores offer seminars and valuable ways of learning the information that you need.

Tell us about your new project called MP3studio.com.

DP: I am in the middle of building a website called MP3studio.com where we will offer on-line training sessions where you will be able to play with virtual products like the Akai MPC or a WarpFactory. All the knobs and buttons will activate the software that will give you hands-on experience with products. Each of these sections will have fast-paced little movies that will guide you through the world of high tech products. We hope it will be fun and informative.

It almost sounds like a virtual recording school. Is this the idea?

DP: Exactly, this type of thing is one of the biggest reasons I came on board with Full Sail. The school is high-tech, as high-tech as it gets. We often are working with manufactures to introduce new products to the students as fast as they are being released.

It sounds like you are a strong MP3 supporter. Do you see any danger of losing control of music as it becomes harder to track?

DP: We cover all these issues at Full Sail including encryption technology and different methods of encoding. But for all the brilliant encryption codes out there, you're going to find just as many who will want to crack it. I guess there will always have to be police be it on horses or on the Internet. I'm not worried about it. I think that MP3 is cheaper than a cassette and it sounds better. I think it offers a tremendous variety of music. I think it's launching a condensed file format trend. I don't know if it will end up as the dominant thing but this is the first and so far the standard.

Recently you produced Mary J. Blige for a Michael Jordan commercial. Can you tell us a bit about how it happened and what sort of equipment you used in the session?

DP: Basically, Michael Jordan is launching his own clothing line called Jordan. He was producing a television commercial to introduce the line and all the athletes that he has signed to his brand. He chose the song "Overjoyed" which we all know as a classic Stevie Wonder composition. Jordan wanted Mary J. Blige to sing the song and it was kind of his way to say to all the artists that he's overjoyed about them representing his brand. So, we started vocal production at Sony studios in New York and we finished all the music and mixed it at Stevie's Wonderland Studios in LA. Basically the approach was to keep it as true to the original as possible but kind of add a little of today's edge to the music.

A foot in the past, a foot in the future. What did you use to create some of the sounds?

DP: Well the Electrix M0-FX was definitely huge. Stevie was there for the session. He's been getting into working with samples and using them off of external drum machines and being able to play them with your fingertips. We took some of the samples and routed them through MO-FX and re-sampled and this is what you hear on the track. Technique wise, we basically sequenced it with Cubase. Stevie is really efficient on Cubase and we also used the Akai MPC limited edition of the new 3000, the re-releases. The Mo-FX was used for drum sweetening. We had Stevie's original master and were able to lock it up to the new sequence. Back in those days, Stevie used a lot of recorded natural sounds. He used stones hitting the ground, birds and Ocean to make percussive grooves. We ran it through MO-FX to give it an updated sound. You know the birds popped out a little more so that you hear them after the beat.

It must be difficult to juggle between teaching and production jobs that arise. Do you have an arrangement with the school that lets you have enough flexibility?

DP: Ya know, the school recognizes this and it has a slogan that says: "Full Sail- *Real World Education*". Being the course director, it's my responsibility to keep my portion of the course up to date. The School recognizes that when I came to Full Sail my career was on the up and up and was becoming bigger. I plan on it being an element for advancing my own experience with film and television production as the school has such advanced equipment. I also really like the idea of trying to start a new generation of people who are getting into the industry who can fully appreciate technical point as well as musical angles. The school recognizes that I bring a lot to the table. Being able to take forays to do this commercial or what ever and then to coming back to explain to a class how something was done is invaluable. To be able to tell them about working with Stevie Wonder and Mary Blige in the studio is a real experience to bring back to the classroom. It gives students an edge, *Real World Experience*. When we did the session at Sony in New York, the assistant engineer was a Full Sail graduate. He was only 2 months into his internship with Sony and there he was working with Stevie Wonder!

Look at groups like the Chemical Brothers who are doing performance mixing. Do you see the role of the producer evolving and changing?
DP: Yes, in fact, I can totally relate. When I first auditioned for Wonder, he was looking for a young producer/programmer to bring new technologies to his studio and to see if there were ways he could find about new devices that were out there that he could learn to operate himself. Stevie also wanted to expand his live show to incorporate what he had been doing in the studio for almost thirty years. He wanted to take his live performance to another level. So, this was probably one of the biggest things that became my responsibility. I worked with Rob Arbiter, who had taken him to a fairly sophisticated level with implementing MIDI and digital audio workstation.

In 1991, I became what would later be called the Digital Music Director on the Natural Wonder Tour. We were actually implementing studio techniques into the live stage show. My responsibility was to make sure that the six keyboards on stage were synced to the computer. We had a thirty-piece orchestra, a nine-piece band, four background singers and Stevie. I had sequences and pre-recorded vocals playing underneath the band, a click track playing to the drummer and the orchestra. We performed for two hours and never did the same show on any given night. If you ever have worked with computers and sequencers, you know that you would prefer to have a set show. But Stevie doesn't work this way so often you'd have 40-some people wondering what to do when Stevie decided to launch into a Lenny Kravitz tune out of the blue. As the Digital Director, I had basically operate like a DJ, go with the flow and be prepared for something new every night.

As a kid growing up in Indiana, I learned to DJ and to rap a bit. The way we would make our mix tapes was crucial to the performance. This experience came in very handy when I started with Stevie's live show although of course everything was far more complex. When I used to DJ, I eventually got tired of doing other people's music so I learned how to create my own. This is part of the growth process.

Every sixty days you have a new batch of students coming into your classroom. You teach them about real life experience and give them training in many technical aspects of the business. In turn, what do you learn from the kids that go through your classes?

DP: I learn the next trend. I see the next dress styles so I can stay hip, you know what I'm sayin'? (Laughs) Everyone coming in here is the next generation and every sixty days it's a completely new generation. I'm giving up my secrets now, but you know this is like what better way to stay on top of technology than to learn all the new things that are coming along right along with the students. I can't think of a better way to see what tomorrow's gonna be and how the technology is going to fit with it.

It seems that music is making a major shift. Barriers are breaking down and mediums are merging. There's really no longer a threat between DJs and Musicians. What kind of music do you see yourself producing in two years? What sort of goals do you have for yourself?

DP: The biggest goal I have right now is to continue with the style that I have been doing. I'm not strictly analog and I'm not strictly digital. I don't use all acoustic instruments and I don't use all Synths and samplers either. I like to keep the mix going. I like to do soundtrack work and I like to do strictly instrumental for dance and club. I think for me, I love the fact that I'm trying to focus on the longevity factor. One of the biggest things that I learned from Stevie Wonder was longevity. The fact is that it's all simply built around the love for music.

I love this whole Internet opportunity. I hope to have an incredible site up over the next two to three years. That's really what it's all about for me, learning to write music for the format, you know computers and the new players. The focus is about using the new format and learning to make my music sound as good off of the Internet as it has on CDs and records. You know by this time next year, this whole MP3 thing is going to be bigger than ever only with video. There are already many independent video and television companies that are focused in this direction. I think that it all represents an amazing amount of opportunities for DJs to work in TV, soundtracks and more.

Artist wise, you know when I first moved down to Orlando, I heard a Chris Fortier Remix of Sara McLaughlin and it blew me away. Now this DJ took a track that I knew from its radio success and put it in the form of a dance track. When I heard that, the top of my head blew off with ideas of how many classics there out there that could have the same treatment. You know, a Lena Horne song. You give a DJ a vocal or an old school track and there is no telling what he could do with it. There's a DJ named DJ Delano who does primarily dance hall reggae stuff. He's the first one to show me that you can take any form of music that's inspirational to you and make if viable to your audience. In the end it's all about vision. Vision to see the possibilities and vision to make your own original statement.

INTERVIEW WITH JOHNNY VICIOUS

Fig. #45: Johnny Vicious

Johnny Vicious is a prolific New York-based producer, remixer and DJ with a style that ranges from hard, percussive house to quixotic garage. Regarded globally as a turntable phenomenon, Vicious has developed an extensive following in the US as well as the UK, France, Japan and Italy. Born and raised in Long Branch, New Jersey, Johnny initially favored rock but by chance began toying with a pair of turntables. "Its funny", Johnny laughs while recollecting his progression, "One minute I was into Motley Crew and the next I was listening to Tony Humphries mix show on Kiss-FM." Slots at Red Zone, Glamorama and Sound Factory Bar eventually led to a residency at the famed Roxy.

After hooking up with Sound Factory Bar's Jeffery Rodman, Johnny formed Vicious Muzik that paved the way for his seminal Liquid Bass EP which showcased his promising melange of beats and samples.

Vicious went on to establish a solid relationship with the owners of the legendary Salsoul Records where he handled promotions for his Synergy Album. Johnny got clearance from the label to Remix some their classic disco titles injecting rousing '90s updates. Over a dozen releases later, his treatment of classic disco anthems from the likes of Loletta Holloway and the Shades of Love led to his in demand status as a producer and remixer. Soon pop notables such as Whitney Houston, Aretha Franklin, Deborah Cox, Jimmy Somerville, Miami Sound Machine, Deee-Lite, Drizabone, Thelma Houston, The O'Jays, Sandra Bernhard, and Traci Lords were seeking Johnny's talents. Ever careful to maintain his underground affiliation, Vicious continues to work with the likes of Loni Clark, Third Nation, Adele and Winter Darling.

"While I'm doing major label mixes, I want to keep myself in the underground", states Johnny. "As a DJ, I always want to hear new records and as a producer, I always want to make new sounds. I don't want to get away from this music. Dance music will always be around and I'll always be a part of it". We caught up to him in his home studio where he has recently completed a brilliant treatment of Simply Red's "It Takes A Lot of Love."

Many DJs aspire to become producers and remixers. How did you begin to develop a technical knowledge from your background as a DJ?
JV: I always needed to know how certain DJs played records and I learned from the best. From that I understood how to use a crossover or filter and how to make a record have more feeling

by filtering. This helped me put a Remix together by knowing when to put a kick in or when to bring the high hats in, its all about the feeling of the record.

You have stated that it is important to learn each piece of gear inside and out before you buy something new. Many hit records have been produced on relatively simple equipment. What was one of your favorite early tools?

JV: My favorite was the Ensoniq 16, it is a keyboard, sampler and sequencer. I did my first 3 records from this keyboard, and only this keyboard, then I soon learned how to MIDI up other equipment to it, and mix out of a 16 track. As I learned the equipment I grew, and bought more.

Were you able achieve release quality tracks from this set up?

JV: Not really, I had to do a lot of mastering and I achieved good quality thanks to Tom Moulton, Rick Essig and Greg Vaughn at Frankfort Wayne mastering labs.

How did your reputation lead to work with the major labels and stars such as Whitney Houston?

JV: Well some of the A&R's of the dance departments are out in the clubs every weekend listening to DJ's play music and once in a while you'll hear one of my songs. Lucky enough they heard my songs and found out my details and called me to do mixes for people like Whitney Houston. I'm glad it was from what I did and not who I knew.

Who were some of your early influences?

JV: Early influences are Todd Terry, David Morales, Jr. Vasquez, Frankie Knuckles, masters at work and Tony Humphries.

Recently, I heard your great sounding Remix of Simply Red's "Ain't That a Lot of Love." Do ever have input from the original artist or is it all up to you? Was the vocal supplied on DAT and you created the rest?

JV: Most of the vocals are supplied on DAT, if the song is too slow or too fast to time stretch you may have to retake the vocals in which it becomes a collaboration between you and the artist. I feel that producer points should be given if this happens. This particular track was given to me on DAT and I did the rest.

Today most studios are comprised of hardware and software. Would you give us an overview of the equipment that you use in production?
JV: Sure, Motu 2408, Pro Tools, Mackie D8B, Rebirth, Virus, Korg 03 RW, Super Nova, JP8080, Raveolution, Studio 5, JP800, CSFX, EPS 16, Glyph 9, dbx de-essers, VT 737, Orbaneq, TLA EQs, MP5, Tannoy system 1000, TB 303, Zoom 9050, Juno 6, Juno 106, DJ 70, Orbi, Audity, Roland vocoder, and the Electrix FilterFactory and the WarpFactory.

Do you record your own vocalists or rely on sampled vocals? What are some of the tricks involved?
JV: Sure, I have recorded many vocals but in the beginning I could only sample, so I did. I record scratch vocals in my studio, get the track sounding banging, and then re-record vocals in a good quality studio. It saves a lot of dollars in recording costs. Sampling opened music wide to be able to put a word or phrase any way, and wherever you want it to be in the track that is the beauty of it.

How do you typically approach a Remix? Do you start with the rhythm tracks, the bassline or melody?
JV: Well, I have a lot personal ideas that I incorporate into the track, either from something I have heard or just a novelty idea I get. Then I try it in the track, if it works then that's great if not then I move on. First I get a rhythm track going then match the vocals up to the beat, if its to slow I time stretch, and then have my keyboard player Mike Nigro come over and make the melody and it usually starts with him playing a few things then I tell him to change it around to where I hear the keyboard lines fitting the vocal. Sometimes he doesn't even recognize what he has played because by the end of the mix I might have changed the whole keyboard line.

How do you feel about programs such as Steinburg Recycle or Sonic Foundry's Acid? Is there a danger of creating a glut of auto-generated grooves?
JV: I have Recycle, and I use it to change drum loops around I love it because it gives me ideas and it adds to the track, it is easier, but if you understand what it is doing it teaches you how to program your own drums and how you like them to sound in the future.

Do you program your own drum patterns and bass lines? Is there an advantage of this method over auto-generated styles?
JV: Yes, but I also use arpeggiation to program some of the drum patterns.

I make one of my keyboards with ARP. I start with the controller and then hook a couple of drum sounds up and see which ARP pattern sounds the best. I do the same for bass lines that get changed around more frequently.

Would you explain the importance of an artist understanding mechanical rights and royalties?

JV: Rights and royalties are very important if you have a big hit, it becomes your bread and butter, some artists retire on their royalties and publishing. Your advance is the quick cash and it is very satisfying, but it only lasts so long, those surplus royalty checks and licensing checks are saviors sometimes. Please go out and read about this subject, then get yourself a good music lawyer that understands about publishing and royalties.

What is the advantage of working with an established publishing company versus publishing your own material?

JV: Well the publishing companies, if they are hungry, will go out and get the money that's due to you, try to find one that's gonna do all of the work for from submitting your work and getting it registered to collecting the actual money. Beware, some are lazy. There's no problem publishing your own work as long as you are aggressive about getting the money yourself and you have the time.

If you were starting out today and knew you had some very hot tracks but no track record, what would be your first move?

JV: Going a record company that has a track record that you like on it then find out the name of the A&R person, call him or her send in the track and if they like it, you're in business. It would be a good idea to send it out to a couple of different labels don't be greedy with the advance, relax its your first track if it is a hit and sells you'll get those royalties you deserve.

Do you feel that producers, such as yourself, get enough credit from other DJs who use your material?

JV: I get e-mails and people calling radio station trying to get my work and wanting to find out what I'm working on all the time. I wish I had the Internet when I started. I would have loved to talk to a few of my idols online and found out how they achieved their goals.

Do you think that MP3 represents an opportunity for new producers or is there a risk of not making anything if your music becomes popular?
JV: It's becomes popular, but you aren't getting paid for having your work spread around the Internet without your permission it might create a hype but when you don't need that hype and want to make money it's a bad thing.

How can you protect your copyright?
JV: From MP3s you can't, you are at the mercy of the bootleggers. Other than that, register it.

Do you think the dance industry is on the brink of becoming over commercialized?
JV: Yes, if the bootlegging of CDs doesn't stop and the mp3 sites don't get shut down, then dance music will get in trouble just like it did seven or eight years ago when there was too much for free and people were making tapes and selling them in bulk. They still are right on Canal St. and on 8th Ave, the same places have been there for years. The industry lost a lot of money. Otherwise it will always be underground at first, then commercialized.

What are your plans for the future?
JV: An album and a mix CD.

It must be difficult to balance your career as a DJ and a producer. How do you split your time?
JV: Well, the weekends are for playing records and the week is to play in the studio.

What is your best piece of advice for an aspiring DJ/remixer?
JV: Get out and do it, don't sit on your ass and wonder and say I wish I could do that if its your passion then do it, I started with nothing just a dream and friends that wanted good music at some house parties, then I developed from there and had another dream to make the records I was playing. If you have a dream, make it a reality.

Do you ever consider outside artists for your own label?
JV: I always use good talent. That's what my album is going to consist of.

Can an aspiring producer contact you? How?
JV: Sure **muzik448@aol.com** and very soon at **johnnyvicious.com.**

Craig Anderton is hard to categorize. He has played Carnegie Hall, recorded three albums with the group Mandrake back in the '60s, coined the term "electronic musician" and created the magazine bearing that name, written 15 books on musical electronics, did session work on home-made drum machines and synthesizers in New York in the '70s, helped mix a CD (Valley in the Clouds by David Arkenstone) that stayed in the new age charts for two years, lectured on technology and the arts in 37 states and 10 countries, started one of the first net sites specifically for musicians (America Online's "Sound, Studio, and Stage"), and designed equipment used by groups such as Boston, Van Halen, Martha Davis (the Motels), and Peter Gabriel keyboardist Larry Fast. He also specified the design for Steinberg's Quadrafuzz software plug-in, and produced three albums by classical guitarist Linda Cohen. Then there's his solo CD, "Forward Motion," which had quite a nice run back in the early '90s.

Now he's taken a turn into electronica, performing in Europe and (far more rarely) in the United States, as well as working on studio releases. His upcoming CD, "Sexy World," (which was being completed as this interview occurred) has already had two Remixes (by BWA) released over in Germany, and four Remixes done at Walnut Studios for an upcoming DTS 5.1 surround sound CD. As if that wasn't enough, "Sexy World" was recorded entirely using Sonic Foundry's Acid software, so he's releasing the loops as a loop library in WAV format.

You've worked with rock, new age, and classical material. What got you into electronica?
CA: I've been into electronic music for a long time, starting with an experimental band called "Anomali" that played in the Philadelphia area around 1970. It wasn't exactly dance music, but would alternate between trancey, psychedelic parts and more rhythm-oriented sections. When groups like Kraftwerk came along a bit later, I thought it was great. I also enjoyed the synthpop bands of the '80s, like Ultravox and Gary Numan, as well as what Miles Davis was doing, and got turned on to "real" techno at EQ Magazine's MIDI Expo in 1991, which is when my music took on more and more of this type of character. So what's happening now is, to me, part of a continuum that continues to grow and expand.

There was a big gap between your new age projects in the '80s and your current forays into dance music. Why the delay?

CA: Although I was doing a lot of techno-type music, I didn't think it was worth putting out. I don't believe in producing music for a particular market. You make the kind of music you want to make, and if lots of other people like it too, then you have a career. If they don't, it doesn't matter, because to me, music is above all about personal discovery and expression. I knew my music wasn't commercially viable and didn't want to waste my time trying to force it down people's throats. But I also loved what I was doing. I have several CDs worth of unreleased material that I did for myself and my friends. That was good enough. One of the things that is so "right" about the current scene is that people sit in small studios, or in their bedrooms, with gear that was rejected by rock musicians a long time ago, and make great music. They make it for themselves, for other people, whatever. I see more love of music and less concern about commercializing it, which means to me that they grasp what music is all about.

What started your re-immersion in the music scene?

CA: It was totally by accident. I was over in Germany covering a press event by CreamWare, when a good friend suggested I see a Cologne musician who goes under the name Dr. Walker. The guy blew me away as much as when I first saw Jimi Hendrix, and believe me, for a guitarist that's saying a lot. He basically plays mixer, drum machine, and synth, usually with other people, and he is a true master of the mixing board. He plays mixer in a physical, visceral way unlike anything I've ever seen. It completely transformed my views of music to see him play, because he was doing live remixing rather than the conventional "let's get these instruments down to two tracks" sort of mixing used in pop records.

He's also part of Syncom Productionz, which produces a huge electronic music party every year in Cologne, Germany called "Battery Park." It goes on for 10 days, or maybe I should say 10 nights and mornings, in a bunch of clubs, and there are dozens of live acts, workshops, and DJs. It's not like a convention, though, it has a much more underground vibe and is really all about the music. Anyway, he invited me to come and check out the festival, and as an afterthought, figured it would be cool if I brought over some little boxes and did a sort of experimental concert at his Liquid Sky club. I said okay, and put together a simple act. But it went over really well, and a bunch of DJs invited me to jam with them on guitar. It has just escalated from there. I go over to Cologne as much as I can, and after a few gigs and Remixes, I felt the time was right to put out another CD.

Guitars aren't usually associated with Electronica. You use guitar a lot in your music, but it sure doesn't sound like guitar. How do you integrate it into your setup?

CA: Well, my live setup is actually very basic: a single Ensoniq ASR-X Pro holds all the sequences and loops. But it's dreadful for live performance, so I use a Peavey PC-1600 fader box to Remix the sequenced loops in real time. No two performances are ever the same; it really depends on the mood of the crowd, as well as my mood. The guitar goes through a Line 6 POD, then my secret weapon, a vocoder. However, the vocoder source isn't a mic, but the rhythm track. When I play with other people, I request an aux send from the drum channels as a source. The ASR-X, vocoded guitar, and processed guitar go to a tiny mixer and from there, to whatever sound system the DJ or club is using. I also do vocals if it's right for the occasion. When the guitar isn't vocoded, it's usually set for rhythmic effects using the POD's tap tempo option. This puts the guitar into a rhythmic groove, which is a necessity for this type of music.

What kind of vocoder do you use?

CA: I've used several over the years: the one I designed for PAIA Electronics, the Synton 202, and the Roland SVC-350. But now I use the Electrix Warp Factory because it's a lot more flexible in terms of sound mutation, and you can play with it in real time. Once I was jamming with a band over in Germany and the cable carrying the straight guitar sound failed. So I ended up playing the vocoder for the whole gig, using the processed guitar. I couldn't have done that with a traditional vocoder.

To put it delicately, you're somewhat older than your audience. Do you find that is a problem?

CA: Not at all. People in the '60s had this "don't trust anyone over 30" mentality that was really stupid. People of the DJ generation are the most open-minded musicians I've seen. That's exactly why the music's so good; they'll mix in 1970s Miles Davis with 1980s Public Enemy with 1990s Fatboy Slim. They don't seem to care about anything other than whether the music moves them or not. Far from giving me a hard time, people like Dr. Walker and others have taken me under their wing and been totally encouraging. Because of them, I can truly say that I've never, ever enjoyed playing music more than I am right now.

Why are you also releasing "Sexy World" as a loop library for Acid?
CA: It's my attempt to make music more interactive. When I play live, I very much key off of the audience, and try to tailor the music for the situation. When I was first approached about doing a CD, I felt there was no way to translate what I do into a "fixed" piece of music – someone might listen to a tune when they're waking up, going to sleep, doing the dishes, when they're angry, when they're happy – you can't interact with the listener the way you can with a live audience, and it's a drag actually.

I thought by putting out the loop library, people would not only have loops for their own music, but if they basically liked my music, they could mess with it as much as they wanted – speed it up, slow it down, replace my vocals, whatever. To test out the concept I got loop libraries into the hands of friends, and got some Remixes back. I loved to hear what people did with the loops. I'm hoping people will send me some of their Remixes, that would be cool.

What about the surround sound project?
CA: Oh, that's another one that came about by accident. The CEO of Above Records, George Daly, has sort of been tracking what I've been doing for the past several years, and he told me he thought some of the cuts on "Sexy World" would be ideal for 5.1 Remixing. George was just starting a label named Flight Records devoted to DTS surround releases, so the timing was good. I had never worked in surround, but he invited me out to one of the label's studios and we gave a go of it, with him doing 95% of the mixing. The bottom line is it seemed like this "virtual" music is just made for surround. For my next project, I want to do some almost classical, Columbia-Princeton type "electronic music" in a 5.1 format, but filtered through the sensibilities of today's trance and techno. I can hardly wait.

Do you have any advice for people new to the field who want to get into the world of live performance dance music?
CA: Sure. Just make sure that whatever you do is completely, 100% from the heart and you can't go wrong. Put your brain on hold and let your emotions speak. And don't be afraid to throw in humor, we all need to smile sometimes. I can't emphasize it enough: play what you want to play, and if you want to turn that into a career, hope that other people also want to hear what you play. But if they don't, it doesn't matter. It's wonderful beyond my wildest dreams that people actually like what I'm doing these days. But if they didn't, I'd still be playing music, even if I was the only audience.

Fig. #47: Rob Hoffman

Rob Hoffman is a producer, engineer, writer, programmer and remixer based in Los Angeles. Rob has worked with many of the industry's most successful artists and producers. His engineering and programming can be heard on records like Michael Jackson's "HIStory" and Quincy Jones' "Q's Jook Joint". Rob, also a talented writer and musician, has a background that encompasses everything from R&B and rock to jungle and house.

In addition to maintaining a busy studio schedule, Rob has found the time to launch his own *Love Groove Records*, an independent label specializing in dance, pop and alternative music. Among his talented roster of artists, Michelle Crispen (Love Groove Records) was the recent winner of the New Artist Discoveries contest at the sixth annual Billboard Dance Music Summit. Her current release, "Superstar," a Robbie Hoffman-produced single with six separate Remixes, is poised to catapult Michelle into the world dance arena.

We caught up to Rob recently at his home studio in Century City, Califorinia.

Rob, You have had an amazing variety of projects in your career. What was your background and how did you get so far at a relatively young age?

RH: I started playing guitar and piano at age ten, and I also played saxophone and trombone in the school band. My friends and I started a band in the sixth grade. I think we played the same five songs for about 3 years. Anyway, I got a little more serious studying jazz and classical guitar in high school and continuing through college. While in college I recorded all the live concerts - orchestra, big band, voice recitals, etc. I was left alone as to how I wanted to record those concerts so I got to experiment quite a bit. It was then that I decided I wanted to go into engineering and production as a career. Those few years of engineering helped me move quickly once I landed a job at a studio. I could read orchestral scores and had a pretty good handle on the process. Within a few months I was thrown into the Michael Jackson "HIStory" project. I went from assisting to engineering and playing keyboards and guitar during that record. A lot of hard work and a little luck.

You have extensive talents in many areas of production, from engineering to writing to remixing. What aspects of production do you enjoy the most?

RH: Everything has its rewards. It's exciting to hear a song come together, or to punch in on an 85 piece orchestra. My mood and who I'm working with very much dictate how I feel about the process. Certainly working with a great vocalist like Christina Aguilera, I just want to record vocals all day.

You did the programming for Michael Jackson's "HIStory". What were some of the tools and instrumentation used in this track?

RH: I was one of the programmers used on the whole record along with an incredible list of talented musicians. We had just about any synth you could ever want. Three synclaviers, mini-moogs everywhere. It was truly a synth museum. We also had access to instruments that weren't available to the general public. I have one of the first Nord Leads, one of the first Prophecy's. We even had the Yamaha VP-1, some crazy $45,000 modeling synth. Primarily everything was sequenced on either the MPC or in Studio Vision. We generally recorded through vintage Neve modules and mixed on the SSL.

Obviously, Michael Jackson has always had a great deal of dance influence in his music. Sequence programming lends itself well to dance production. How do you approach a dance groove versus a straight-ahead production?

RH: The only real difference would be in the initial palette of sounds I pull up. For a ballad I generally fill my samplers with orchestral sounds, whereas on a R&B or dance groove they might get filled with drum samples and loops. I pretty much start with some kind of 4 or 8 bar groove and build the song around that. Later I expand the groove, building transitions and adding parts.

It must be very interesting working with the legendary Quincy Jones. How did you develop this relationship? Would you tell us about the "Q's Jook Joint" project?

RH: After "HIStory" I was heavily involved with Bruce Swedien. He kept me working with him. In general I'd start out assisting him on a project and within a few days I'd be playing keyboards and engineering overdubs in another room or in his room after he went home for the day. That's how the Quincy project came about. Bruce hired me and each night he would go home and I would stay up with Quincy and Rod Temperton engineering and programming until Bruce came back the next morning. I didn't sleep much.

Working with Quincy and Rod was amazing. These guys have created some of the most magical musical moments ever. And of course working on a Quincy project the cast of musicians is out of this world.

You seem to be getting heavily involved with dance music with your own artist Michelle Crispen (Love Groove Records) and recently with your work with Christina Aguilera. Is this a new focus?

RH: I never want to be pigeon holed. I love working on all kinds of music and I listen to everything. Dance is pretty much where Michelle wanted to go as an artist so I was happy to explore that. Dance music for me has fewer restrictions than say R&B or pop. Traditionally in R&B you're limited in your sounds and production style to what's hot on the charts and radio. In dance music you can pretty much go where you want as long as it grooves. As a producer it's a very freeing experience. As for Christina, my partner and I wrote and produced the demo that led to her record deal. After producing the big power-ballad for the debut album we've done a Remix for her and are starting to write for her next record.

Would you tell us about "Love Groove Records"? How did it come about? You seem to be very busy as an independent engineer and producer. Why develop your own label as well?

RH: Love Groove was basically started to help promote the artists that I'm developing. Not every artist needs a major label deal and Love Groove is an outlet for that. It's an incredible amount of work and a whole new side of the business for me. But now with each new artist I work with I have the option of shopping them to a major or releasing them on my own. Each method has its place depending on style of music and the artist's expectations.

How did you get into remixing? How do you approach a Remix versus a regular production?

RH: My first Remixes were for Michael Jackson, mainly for the videos and tours. To me Remixes are much easier than writing a song from scratch. The hook is there, the vocal production is done. You pretty much have a roadmap. It's just up to the Remixer to make the scenery interesting. I generally listen to the original mix, get a feel for what the artist is saying. Then I decide how close I want to stick to the arrangement. From there I figure out tempos; the original tempo, and then how far away I want to go. Then I'll start building the groove with maybe the chorus vocals as a guide. From there the arrangement starts to fall into place. As I expand the song form I drop in the verse vocals, figure out where my breaks are going to go, and try to give DJ's places to get in and out of the mix.

Do you need to have a music background to Remix?

RH: It helps. There's no right way to do it. But certainly knowing if you're in the right key is a good thing. It bothers me when people say you have to be a DJ to do Remixes or that you have to be a musician. A great musician can adapt and can bring a different approach to a Remix that your average DJ isn't going to think of. At the same time a good DJ will bring different ideas to the table because he isn't bound by any preconceived musical rules.

What are the basic tools that you use in a Remix? Software? Hardware?

RH: I've been using Studio Vision since the very beginning, lately in conjunction with Pro Tools. As Studio Vision fades into obscurity I'll either switch to Pro Tools 5.0 (if they can get the MIDI stuff as happening as SV) or Cubase or Logic. The thought of switching sequencers is daunting. I have about 30 synths, the Mackie D8B digital console, a nice collection of foot pedals and outboard gear. I use the standard software tools like Recycle, as well as plugins and some shareware sound manglers.

Often a remixer is supplied with a dry vocal on a DAT. Is this where you start or do you have access individual parts on the original multi track?
RH: Whenever I can I try to get the multitracks. This really gives me the most leeway on a Remix. But in most cases I simply get the acapella vocal on a DAT. It also depends on how close the label wants me to stay to the original song. If they want me to just alter the mix, kind of a dance/pop radio mix I ask for all the elements. If they have no idea or want me to take it someplace really different, then I just need the vocals.

Often a release has multiple remixed versions. Is a specific style targeted in the Remixes or is it more the quantity approach, hit and miss?
RH: Every label has their own idea about Remixes. Some really know the market and can target specific remixers and styles. Others have no idea and are just hiring remixers based on peer recommendations.

You have are beginning to write a Remix column for Keyboard Magazine. What are some of the areas that you want to discuss?
RH: I think people who isolate themselves within a particular genre of music have some general assumptions about how their music and other genres of music are created. Because I work in so many different styles I want to talk about the differences and how my work on R&B/pop records influences my dance records and vice versa.

It's interesting to see elements of dance music making there way into pop and rock music with the use of 909 drum machines, vocoders and filters. Do you think there is a danger of the genre becoming too commercialized? Where is it headed?
RH: There's always that danger. But for someone like me who loves working in all genres and mixing up production styles and techniques it's a great time to be making music. Dance music has never really been accepted in America the way it is in Europe, even though some of our biggest hits are dance songs. So I hope to see more acceptance of dance music by the industry. It always amazes me when a major label tells me they're not into signing a dance artist yet the only hit they've had on

the charts that year was a Remix of their pop or R&B act. We're all trying to make a living making music. I'll be pretty happy if one of my Remixes makes it to the top ten on the pop charts. I don't see success as selling out.

What are you working on currently?
RH: We're finishing up Michelle's album and looking for the next project for Lovegroove. We have several Remixes lined up and of course we're submitting songs to established artists on a continual basis. We're also working on Heather Holley's music, she's my writing partner. We've been working together for 4 years now. We're also developing a couple different artists in the pop vein.

What's the plan for Love Groove Records?
RH: We've just signed a new distribution deal. So we'll be getting Michelle's record out in the next few months. I'm trying to find another artist to sign to Lovegroove, something that compliments what we've already done and can benefit from the contacts we've developed.

Are you approachable? That, is can anyone send you material for consideration?
RH: Of course, I'm always looking.

How can you be contacted?
RH: The Internet is the easiest route; **robmix@earthlink.net** or the website **http://www.lovegrooverecords.com**